SHANGHAI

Addresses in this book are given in *pinyin: dajie* is a main thoroughfare (sometimes translated as 'avenue'); *lu* is a road and *jie* is a street; *xiang* and *long* both denote an alley or lane. Chinese characters for names and addresses of hotels, restaurants and shops are provided in the listings under 'Practical Information'. Names of all the sights and other places described in the book are also given in simplified Chinese characters in the Index.

SHANGHAI

Lynn Pan, May Holdsworth and Jill Hunt
Revised by Peter Hibbard

PASSPORT BOOKS
a division of *NTC Publishing Group*
Lincolnwood, Illinois USA

Published by Passport Books in conjunction with
The Guidebook Company Ltd, Hong Kong
THIRD EDITION 1995

This edition first published in 1992 by Passport Books, a division of NTC Publishing Group,
4255 W. Touhy Avenue, Lincolnwood (Chicago), Illinois 606-46-1975, USA,
originally published by The Guidebook Company Ltd

Library of Congress Catalog Card Number:

Grateful acknowledgement is made to the following authors and publishers for
permission granted:

Andre Deutsch Ltd and Les Editions Gallimard for *The Long March* by Simone de Beauvoir

Victor Gollancz Ltd and Simon & Schuster for *Empire of the Sun* by J G Ballard © 1984

Random Century Group for *In the People's Republic* by Orville Schell © 1977

Watson, Little Ltd for *Dreaming in a Shanghai Restaurant* by D J Enright

Grove Press and HarperCollins (UK) Ltd for *Life and Death in Shanghai* by Nien Cheng © 1986

Chatto & Windus and HarperCollins USA for *Jesting Pilate: The Diary of a Journey* by Aldous Huxley ©
1926 Mrs Laura Huxley

The Estate of Vicki Baum for *Shanghai '37* by Vicki Baum © 1939 Lert Family Trust

Simon & Schuster for *Mandate of Heaven* by Orville Schell © 1994

Victor Gollancz for *Red Azalea* by Anchee Min © 1993

Additional material supplied by Peter Hibbard
Editor, Photographic Editor & Designer: John Oliver
Editorial Assistant: Lisa Ottiger
Cover design: Harvey Symons
Map Design: Bai Yiliang and Tom Le Bas

PHOTOGRAPHY: Magnus Bartlett: 102; Anthony Cassidy: 62; China Guides Series: 29, 86; Department
of Kuomingtang Party History, Taipei: 76; Richard Dobson: 21 (bottom), 128; gang Feng Wang: 45;
Peter Hibbard: 120, 138; HK Museum of History: 21 (top); Hongkong & Shanghai Banking Corporation:
47; Illustrated London News: 78-79, 101; Leung Wai: 28, 41 (top), 51, 82, 87 (bottom); Sarah Lock: 28
(top), 41 (bottom), 87 (top), 121; James Montgomery: cover, 4–5, 36, 37, 106, 116; John Warner Publi-
cations: 120–1; Wattis Fine Art: 13; Jacky Yip: 61; Zhang Ling: 67

Production House: Twin Age Limited, Hong Kong
Printed in Hong Kong by Sing Cheong Printing Co Ltd

(preceding pages) Bridges across the busy Huangpu River link the Shanghai of old with that of the future

Contents

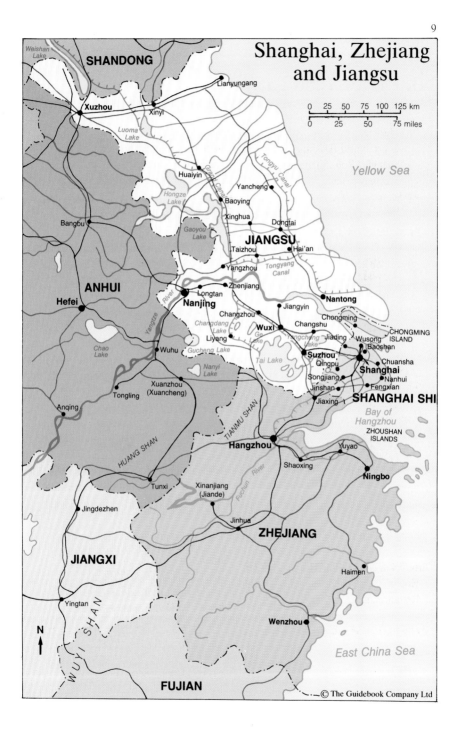

Shanghai, Zhejiang and Jiangsu

Weishan Lake

SHANDONG

Lianyungang

Xuzhou
Xinyi

Luoma Lake

| 0 | 25 | 50 | 75 | 100 | 125 km |

| 0 | 25 | 50 | 75 miles |

Huaiyin

Grand Canal

Tongyu Canal

Yellow Sea

Hongze Lake

Yancheng
Baoying
Xinghua
Dongtai

Bangbu

Gaoyou Lake

JIANGSU

Taizhou
Hai'an

ANHUI

Yangzte River

Yangzhou

Tongyang Canal

Zhenjiang

Longtan

Hefei

Nanjing

Changzhou
Jiangyin

Nantong

Changdang Lake

Wuxi
Changshu

Chongming

CHONGMING ISLAND

Chao Lake

Liyang

Ge Lake

Yangcheng Lake

Jiading
Wusong
Baoshan

Wuhu
Gucheng Lake

Tai Lake

Suzhou
Qingpu

Chuansha

Nanyi Lake

Songjiang
Jinshan

Shanghai
Nanhui
Fengxian

Xuanzhou (Xuancheng)

Jiaxing

SHANGHAI SHI

Tongling

Bay of Hangzhou

Anqing

TIANMU SHAN

ZHOUSHAN ISLANDS

HUANG SHAN

Hangzhou
Yuyao

Shaoxing

Ningbo

Tunxi

Xinanjiang (Jiande)

Fuchun River

Jingdezhen

Jinhua

ZHEJIANG

JIANGXI

Haimen

Yingtan

WUYI SHAN

N

Wenzhou

East China Sea

FUJIAN

© The Guidebook Company Ltd

Shanghai Yesterday And Today   *—Lynn Pan and Peter Hibbard*

Shanghai has its genesis as China's pre-eminent trading centre in the First Opium War, which ended in 1842 with the defeated Chinese empire agreeing to the opening of five Treaty Ports—Shanghai, Canton, Ningbo, Fuzhou and Amoy—to foreign trade and residence. To be a treaty port was to have foreign firms like Jardine Matheson and BAT (British American Tobacco), to have a racecourse, clubs, Sikh policemen, Gilbert and Sullivan at the Amateur Dramatic Club, Lea and Perrin's sauce, and to be visited regularly by British, and occasionally American, gunboats.

In the British and American International Settlement and the French Concession—areas specifically set aside in Shanghai for foreign residence—local administration, from police and sanitation to roads and building regulations, was in foreign hands. The Municipal Council, the governing body of the International Settlement, was dominated by a largely British inner circle representing business interests.

Shanghai became one of the most cosmopolitan cities the world had ever known: the whole gamut of Western and Asian humanity was there, from Jewish tycoons and self-styled White Russian 'countesses' to Annamese gendarmes and Filipino band leaders. One shopped at Hall and Holtz; Lane, Crawford and Company; Laidlaw and Company; and Kelly and Walsh. One read the *North China Daily News*, *Shanghai Times*, *Shanghai Mercury*, *L'Echo de Chine*, *Der Ostasiatische Lloyd*, and the *Shanghai Nippo*. One danced in the chic ballroom of the Cercle Sportif Français and partied at cabarets like the Casanova, Del Monte and Ciro's.

The city's gaiety and stylishness earned it the name of 'Paris of the Orient'. An English visitor to the city in the inter-war period caught its ambiance nicely when he described a woman he saw sitting alone in a nightclub: dressed all in green, she held a green cigarette between her lips and had a glass of crème de menthe on the table in front of her. On other nights, she would be seen in red velvet, sipping cherry brandy and smoking a rose-coloured cigarette.

For a long time the Europeans kept Chinese people out of their parks, clubs and home. Commercially, though, they were on far closer terms, their business transactions channelled through the compradore. Trade and manufacturing grew in leaps and bounds, and Shanghai became the gateway of China—a conduit through which merchandise and ideas were funnelled from the Western world.

One of these ideas was Marxism. A burgeoning proletariat, dismal working conditions in the textile factories, the frankly racist attitudes of many of the Europeans, the immunity from Chinese law provided by the self-governing foreign enclaves—all these factors help towards an explanation of why the Chinese Communist Party was founded in Shanghai. The magazine *New Youth*, edited by Chen Duxiu, is a historical reflection of the forum of debate raging in Shanghai at the time, with its discussions of democracy, education, sexual equality and empirical science. Lu Xun, the Chinese Chekhov, first appeared in these pages. This intellectual, political and social movement was brought to Beijing around 1919, and undoubtably aided China's inexorable move from Confucianism, turmoil and the foreign yoke towards the events that led to the proclamation of the People's Republic of China on October 1, 1949, led by a former assistant librarian at the University of Beijing—Mao Zedong.

When Communism overtook Shanghai in 1949, the city's notorious past was held against it, and the new regime did its best to turn it from what it considered as a Sodom and Gomorrah into a monument to Stalinist central planning. Economically Shanghai was a great success: for years its industrial output and productivity were the highest in the country. With a hundredth of China's population, it accounted for a fourth of the nation's export earnings and a sixth of the national revenue. The city's urban population is just under seven million, but the Municipality of Shanghai, an administrative division encompassing large tracts of the surrounding countryside, has jurisdiction over 13 million people.

Until recently, Shanghai had been starved of investment, Beijing having siphoned off much of its huge earnings. When China began to reform her economic system and opened her doors to the outside world, in the late 1970s, one imagined a resurgence of the entrepreneurial spirit in Shanghai. But this did not quite happen. Shanghai could hardly make the best of the winds of change when it had been left with roads, housing and factories dating back to the 1930s and 1940s. And the more the urban pressures grew, as the streets got more congested and the housing shortage more desperately acute, the more intransigent the general mood became.

For years Shanghai was at cross-purposes with Beijing: once it was too capitalist, then it was too 'leftist'. Its past reputation as a Paradise of Adventurers did not endear it to China's leaders; nor did its association with the Gang of Four, who used it as their base during the Cultural Revolution. Worse still, the Shanghainese are arrogant, and will not be told what to do by anyone, least of all by their masters in Beijing!

Relations with Beijing are still uneasy. Yet, with the passing of the 1980s Shanghai spirited towards a new era of development. Since 1992 the city has experienced a frenzy of activity reminiscent of the heady speculative years of the 1930s, when the 'Paris of the East' came of age. Shanghai is again in the throes of a physical, economic and social revolution destined to restore the city's former status as an international centre of trade, finance and culture.

Ambitious reconstruction programmes are well underway. Already two bridges and two tunnels, traversing the hectic Huangpu River, link the old Shanghai with that of the future. More tunnels and bridges are planned. A new ring road circles the city and new highways and flyovers climb over the clogged and cluttered avenues.

Shanghai's History Through Its Names

When the Chinese want to be literary, or brief, they call Shanghai 'Hu'. The name bespeaks Shanghai's origins as a fishing village, for *hu* is a bamboo fishing device, used during the third century by the people who lived around the Songjiang River (which was subsequently renamed Wusong River, and which forms the upper reaches of the Suzhou Creek). Shanghai is also sometimes known as Chunshen—or Shen for short—because in the third century BC, at the time of the Warring States (475–221 BC), the site on which the city now stands was a fief of the Lord Chunshen, prime minister to the King of the State of Chu. Another name with which Shanghai is associated is Huating. This was a county established in 751, over an area which covers part of present-day Shanghai.

Shanghai took its name from the Shanghai River, a tributary, long since gone, of the Songjiang. A township sprang into being on the west bank of the river, as, recognising its natural advantages as a port, junks and ships came to berth there. This was Shanghai, which presently became the largest town in Huating County. In 1292, Shanghai and four other towns in Huating were brought together to form the County of Shanghai. It was at about this time that the Songjiang was renamed the Wusong River.

But today when most Chinese think of Shanghai, they think not so much of the Wusong as of the Huangpu River. Shanghai's qualifications as a deep water port were greatly improved when a canal—forming that part of the Huangpu downstream of Waibaidu Bridge—was dredged and widened in the fourteenth century. Ships crowded the wharves of Shanghai, and the port itself grew in size and importance, thriving off the trade in cotton and other goods between the coast and the inland provinces on the Yangzi (Yangtse) River.

These were the foundations upon which the Western powers built when, with the opening of Shanghai as a Treaty Port, they came and carved out their enclaves there. The first of the foreign settlements, the British Concession, was bounded on the east along the Huangpu River by the Bund (today's Zhongshan Dong Yi Lu), on the west by Yu Ya Ching Road (today's Xizang Zhong Lu), and on the south by the Yangjingbang Creek (which, after it was filled, was named Avenue Edward VII and which is now called Yan'an Dong Lu). The creek separated the British from the French Concession; the latter started from a wedge between the British Concession and the old Chinese city, and then ballooned out to a large area to the southwest of the city. To the north of the Suzhou Creek, in the district known then and now as Hongkou, lay the American Concession. This was later merged with the British Concession to form the International Settlement.

In the British Concession, the streets spread out behind the Bund in a grid. The main thoroughfare, Nanking Road (Nanjing Lu), ran eastwards from the Bund. The streets parallel to it were named after China's other cities (such as Canton, Fuzhou and Ningbo), while those which ran perpendicular to it (i.e north-south) were named after the provinces (such as Henan, Sichuan and Zhejiang). There was no mistaking the French Concession, because most of the streets there had French names: Rue Lafayette, Avenue Foch, to name but two. The smartest was Avenue Joffre (today's Huaihai Lu), which was to the French Concession what Nanking Road was to the British. Needless to say, these were all renamed when the Communists took over.

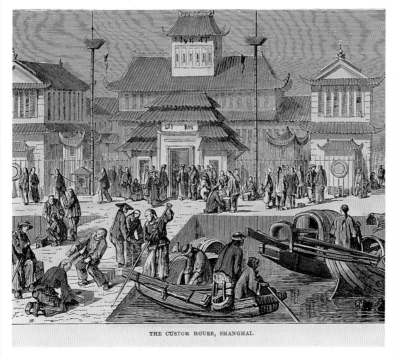

THE CUSTOM HOUSE, SHANGHAI.

The Custom House in Shanghai

Below ground the first artery of the metro system moves the masses to their workplaces. The People's Square, formerly part of the racecourse, has been redeveloped as a home for the city government; whilst the Bund, one of the most famous waterfronts in the East, has been renovated and now awaits a new career. The outdated fabric of Shanghai, largely untouched since the 1940s, is now eagerly felt, folded and cut by the property speculator and business manager in pursuit of efficiency and profit.

The former main streets of the International Settlement and the French Concession are changing beyond recognition. Coloured and neon lights create avenues of enticement for the wealthier modern Shanghainese, whilst modern buildings arise from the ashes of the past at a hungry speed. Reassuringly the government vows that the best of the old will be preserved.

Across from the Bund the Oriental Pearl TV Tower soars into the sky, marking the Pudong New Area as the city of the future. With a foundation of commerce and finance, a new metropolis will materialise in the coming years. Strangely, many of the current changes in the city would appear familiar to the 1930s foreign resident returning today. A sense of déjà vu might prevail despite the bodily change the city continues to bear.

The solitude of the night is now broken by a flourishing entertainment industry ranging from all night discos to ballroom dances; old-time jazz, amateur dramatics staged in Art Deco theatres to grandiose symphony concerts. The gap between rich and poor is manifest, as the Shanghai elite garbed in international designer clothes patronise expensive private clubs and consume the best cognac with a passion.

The old cumshaw, or tip, is gaining a new acceptance and service charges on basic hotel rates, a practice outlawed by the Nationalists in 1945, have returned. Though coffee shops with European style pastries have never fallen from fashion, Western food is back; albeit in the global guise of the ubiquitous fast food franchise. Gambling fever, spurred by the novelty of the Shanghai Stock Market, molests the most innocent Shanghai citizen—and prostitution, a growing phenomenon in China, has been officially recognized as a fact of life.

The growing foreign business and diplomatic communities frequent their own social and sports clubs. The Hongqiao (Hungjao) district, a favoured domicile of foreign capitalists in the 1930s, is again sprouting luxurious private villas and foreign estates. Property speculation is rife and amongst the stores of the Huaihai Lu (Avenue Joffre) and the Nanjing Lu (Nanking Road) can be found a vast array of international goods. On the Nanjing Lu, the Sincere department store, first seen in Shanghai in 1916, has opened a new store close to the original building. Meanwhile the Bund awaits the return of some of its former foreign occupants. Some people might say that Shanghai hasn't really changed over the years very much at all.

Facts For The Traveller

Entering And Leaving Shanghai

By Air

■ **From Hong Kong**: The Hong Kong airline Dragonair has two daily flights to Shanghai, with an additional flight on Saturday. The Shanghai-based China Eastern Airlines has up to six flights each day. Flying time is around two hours.

■ **From the US and Canada**: Air China offers three flights a week from New York and San Francisco. China Eastern offers up to three flights a week from Los Angeles and up to five flights a week from Seattle, as well as two flights a week from Chicago. United Airlines has daily flights from San Francisco and Northwest Airlines have a weekly flight from Seattle. Air China has twice weekly flights from Vancouver as do Canadian Airlines, who resumed operations in 1994.

■ **From Europe**: Air China has a weekly flight from Paris and Frankfurt. China Eastern operates weekly flights from Madrid and Brussels. Initiated in 1994, Lufthansa has twice weekly flights from Frankfurt.

■ **From the Far East**: China Eastern has daily flights from Tokyo and twice weekly flights from Nagasaki, and flies to Shanghai five times a week from Nagoya, as well as up to seven times a week from Osaka. Japan Air Lines fly six times a week from Tokyo, up to six times a week from Osaka and have a weekly flight from Nagasaki. Singapore Airlines operates daily flights from Singapore, Korean Air fly three times a week from Seoul and Philippine Airlines fly three times a week from Manila. China Eastern operates three times a week from Singapore.

Competition between domestic and international airlines for international routes has reached a frenzy and there was a 40% increase in international flights over the 1993-1994 period. Thus the above schedules are subject to change and it is advisable to confirm timetables with your travel agent or the airlines themselves. A list of airline offices in Shanghai is to be found on page 151.

■ HONGQIAO INTERNATIONAL AIRPORT

All flights to Shanghai arrive at the strikingly refurbished Shanghai Hongqiao International Airport, 15 kilometres (8 miles) from downtown. The separate domestic and international terminals are within walking distance of each other, and offer similar services.

The domestic terminal has shops, long-term luggage storage (open 6 am–8 pm; costs double each day after the third day) and a restaurant and bar (open 6 am– 7:30 pm) inside the check-in area. The more impressive international terminal has a

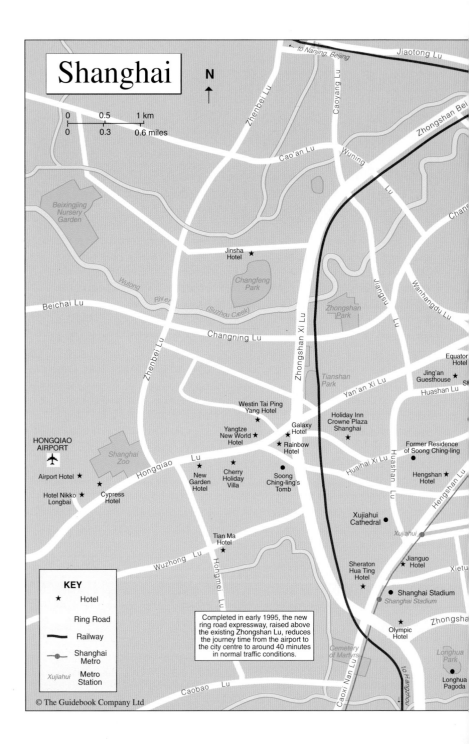

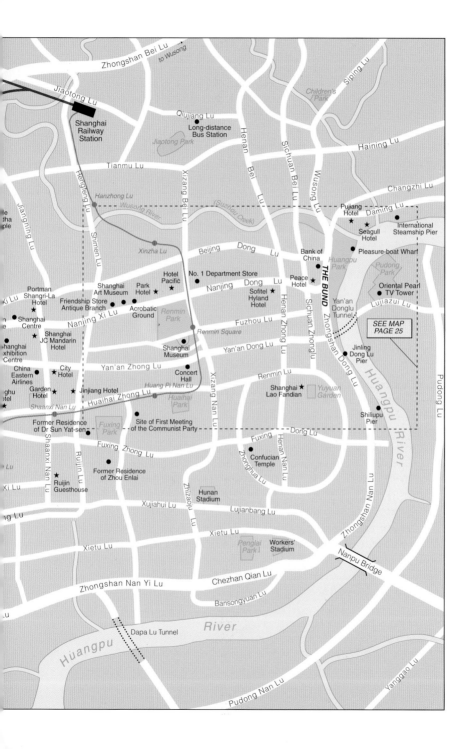

bank for foreign exchange transactions (inside the check-in area for arrivals and departures), long-term luggage storage, bookstore, duty-free shop, lost-and-found, food and gift shops, two restaurants outside the check-in area and a snack bar inside.

Luggage carts are available near the luggage carousels for 4 *yuan* or the equivalent in foreign currency. Porters charge 8 *yuan* per bag and are not supposed to accept tips. A similar service is available at curbside at the two terminals.

There are taxi queues immediately outside the terminals. The fare between the airport and downtown costs around 30 *yuan* and takes from 30 minutes to over one hour, depending on traffic; plan on the latter from 7:30 am–7:30 pm. Numerous hotels also operate a shuttle bus service. If leaving Shanghai by air remember to keep aside some local currency for the departure tax, which stands at present at 25 *yuan* for domestic flights and 90 *yuan* for international flights.

A recorded information service covering schedules and airline information is available in English, Chinese and Japanese by telephoning 268-8918 or 253-7664. Due to heavy bookings on some routes it is essential to reconfirm ongoing and/or return international domestic flights as soon as possible.

By Ship

Two sister passenger/cargo liners, the *Shanghai* and the *Haixing,* sail between Hong Kong and Shanghai, each making two return journeys a month. The 10,000 tonne vessels, launched in 1980, offer five classes of accommodation from special class two-berth cabin to dormitory. Both cruisers feature a library, a swimming pool, video games room, cinema, dance hall and *mahjong* room in addition to a bar, lounge and coffee shop. Western and Chinese food is available in the ships' restaurants. A one-way trip to Shanghai takes around 65 hours and prices range from US$125 for a place in a 5 berth cabin to around US$210 in special classes. It is simplest to book your passage through the China Travel Service (CTS) in Hong Kong, who can also provide return tickets at discounted prices.

One-way tickets from Shanghai to Hong Kong are best purchased through one of the multi-service departments of the China International Travel Service (CITS). Costs are slightly less than those from Hong Kong. Passengers disembark at the International Passenger Terminal at 1 Taiping Lu, to the east of Shanghai Mansions.

There are also weekly sailings to Osaka, Kobe and Yokohama in Japan. The journey, across the Yellow Sea, takes around 23 hours and, again, tickets can easily be purchased through CITS Shanghai or Jinjiang Tours.

Travel To Other Parts Of China

Shanghai is a major hub for air, rail, bus and waterborne transport. Competition between airlines is intense and all 27 airlines in China fly in and out of Shanghai.

China Eastern Airlines have a 40% share of the city air transport market. There is now a greater variety of options available than ever before with, for instance, up to 13 flights a day to Beijing. There is a standard fare for Chinese and foreigners on domestic airlines and bookings can be made at many hotels, through CITS, or at the airline office itself. It is advisable to book as much in advance as possible, since the Chinese are becoming increasingly air-conscious and many seats are group booked.

Everyday 76 trains run to or from the other major cities in China, and there has been a recent increase in the number of trains to neighbouring tourist cities such as Suzhou, as well as the introduction of express double-decker trains. However tickets on major routes are best booked at least three days in advance for Soft (First) class seating or berths. This can be done at many hotels, or through CITS at the railway station (least desired option). On short journeys it is possible to get a hard seat or standing ticket without advance booking.

Towns in Shanghai's outskirts can be reached by bus, for which there are two stations—the Northern Bus Station on Gonghexin Lu (for Jiading) and the Western Bus Station on Caoxi Bei Lu (for Qingpu, Songjiang, Jiading, Jinshan). Buses for destinations further afield (Hangzhou and Huangshan, for example) leave from the Long-distance Station at the junction of Qiujiang Lu and Gingxing Lu.

Visas

Individual visas can be obtained at Chinese embassies and consulates and certain travel agencies in your respective countries; from the Chinese Ministry of Foreign Affairs visa office in Hong Kong (the cheapest way); or through several Hong Kong travel agents including branches of CITS and CTS. Although a visa application can be processed in Hong Kong on the same day the cost will be considerably higher than an application made two or three days in advance. CITS also charge US citizens at a higher rate than many other nationals. For a standard three month visa a passport-sized photograph is all that is required. Requests for visa extensions can be made in Shanghai at the Public Security Bureau.

Tourists travelling in a group enter China on a group visa—a single document listing all members of the group. The visa is obtained by the tour operator on behalf of his clients, and individual passports are not usually stamped—though you can try!

An application for a business visa should generally be accompanied by an invitation from the appropriate host organization in China. In Hong Kong, all that is needed is a letter from the applicant's company confirming that he will travel to China on business. Multiple re-entry visas are available for regular business travellers.

Customs

The ordinary visitor is no longer required to complete a customs declaration form on arrival. There is no limit on the amount of foreign currency that can be taken in, though those holding more than US$5000 (or equivalent) *in cash* should make a declaration. Visitors carrying goods or samples for business purposes and those with unaccompanied baggage should also make a declaration. Customs forms should be kept safely and handed in on departure.

1.5 litres of alcohol over 12% proof, 400 cigarettes (or 100 cigars), unlimited film and medicines for personal use may be taken in free of duty. Receipts for legitimate antiques, which carry a red wax seal, and for gold and silver goods should be kept in case inspection is required on leaving China.

Money

CHINESE CURRENCY

To the great benefit of the visitor, China abandoned its infamous dual currency system in early 1994. The Foreign Exchange Certificate (FEC), for years the tourist 'funny money', has disappeared and the black market for US dollars has waned.

The People's Currency, or Renminbi as it is known, is now the common form of exchange for foreigners as well as Chinese citizens. The basic unit of Chinese currency is the *yuan*; or *kuai* as it is commonly referred to. The yuan is divided into ten *jiao* (often called *mao*), and each *jiao* is divided into ten *fen*. There are large notes for 100, 50, 10, 5, 2 and 1 *yuan*, smaller notes for 5, 2 and 1 *jiao*, and even smaller notes for the 5, 2 and 1 *fen*. Coins are also in circulation for all corresponding values up to 1 *yuan*—though no 2 *jiao* coin exists.

Hard currencies can now be conveniently exchanged into Renminbi at hotels, large stores and branches of the Bank of China. All major European, American and Japanese traveller's cheques are accepted, and these are changed at a slightly better rate than cash. Renminbi can be obtained via credit card at some hotels, though a hefty surcharge is levied. The Bank of China offers the best service to holders of major credit cards subject to a minimum exchange of 800 Rmb. American Express card-holders can obtain Renminbi and traveller's cheques by using the ATM on the 1st floor of the Shanghai Centre. Citibank provides a 24 hour Renminbi ATM Service on the ground floor of the Peace Hotel on the Bund. This two-machine centre also offers fund transfers and balance enquiry services. Hong Kong issued Citibank Visa and Diners Club may also be used.

The Bund in 1932 contrasts vividly with the same scene in 1995

Up to 50% of the total amount of Renminbi obtained may be reconverted to hard currency on leaving China, providing exchange receipts covering the amount are shown. For those travelling on to Hong Kong, Renminbi can easily be converted to Hong Kong dollars at numerous money changers without the need for receipts. In 1994 the US dollar was worth around 8.5 *yuan*—a 50% appreciation over its 1993 FEC value.

FOREIGN CURRENCY

If you need more cash during your stay, one way to get it is to have money wired in your name to the local main branch of the Bank of China. The remittance will arrive in four to six working days. Alternatively a substantial cash advance on your credit card can be drawn at the Bank of China on the Bund. American Express card holders may cash personal cheques up to US$1000 (green/corporate card) or US$5000 (gold card) every 21 days on payment of a service charge.

CREDIT CARDS

China is experiencing a credit card boom, with an estimated 100 million cards being issued by Chinese banks by the year 2000. This development should widen the use of international credit cards at retail outlets. At present international credit cards are widely accepted at designated tourist restaurants and stores as well as at most tourist hotels. However, they are of little value for main street shopping, though they are quickly gaining acceptance at Shanghai's new breed of luxury stores, international boutiques and emporiums.

TIPPING

Although tipping is, in theory, forbidden it has become an accepted and expected practice in many sectors of the hospitality industry. Tipping has become particularly routine in hotels. It is also becoming more prevalent in restaurants and bars. Some taxi drivers will also accept tips. For group tourists tipping of drivers and guides is an obligatory practice.

Local Time

Amazingly for a entire country measuring some 4,300 kilometres (over 2,500 miles) from east to west, the whole of China operates completely within one time zone, eight hours ahead of GMT and 13 hours ahead of EST; although in practice the far northwest of China operates three hours behind Shanghai. Daylight saving, however, is not practised in China.

Travel Agencies

Most foreigners coming to China will have contact with CITS (China International Travel Service), which hosts most group tours and offers individual tour and ticketing services. CTS (China Travel Service), though originally set up to deal with overseas Chinese and Chinese 'compatriots', now deals with all foreigners in much the same way as CITS. In 1989 new state-owned 'Grade A' travel agencies were set up, again with functions similar to CITS. In Shanghai local/regional tours and requests for ship, train and air tickets can be handled by any of the above agencies.

The Shanghai Municipal Tourism Administration, though largely involved with the management of group tourism, does publish useful guides and directories—which are sometimes found in hotel rooms. It also endorses the free quarterly publication *Welcome to China, Shanghai*, which gives valuable tourist information and is available at many hotels.

Communications

International Direct Dialling is available in nearly all tourist hotels between Shanghai and most countries in the world. The same hotels also have business centres providing the standard photocopying, telex and facsimile services. Many hotel lobbies now have card telephones for IDD and local calls. Phone cards cost 20Rmb upwards. The AT&T USA Direct Service is available by dialling 10811. The central branch of the Shanghai Telegraph Office (24 hour service) and the Shanghai Telecommunications Bureau service office (open 7 am–10.30 pm) offer such facilities as long-distance calls, telegrams, telex and facsimile. Addresses are listed on page 151.

China's own English-language newspaper, *China Daily*, is available at most hotels, as is the informative bi-weekly edition of the *Shanghai Star*. The bigger hotels stock the *International Herald Tribune*, *Asian Wall Street Journal*, *USA Today*, *South China Morning Post* and other international newspapers and magazines.

Packing Checklist

Most hotels in Shanghai have a shop that stocks a fairly wide range of international toiletries, as well as food and both alcoholic and soft drinks. There are now branches of the large Hong Kong drug store 'Watsons' in Shanghai and international products are also available in the Friendship Store.

The electricity supply is 220 volts and hotels have a wide variety of socket types, though many provide adaptors for British and American plugs.

Standard 100 ASA colour film is cheap and widely available. Most other types and brands of film are available at selected outlets. It is probably best to ensure that you bring enough batteries with you for your particular photographic requirements.

If you wear glasses, or contact lenses, bring your prescription and a spare pair. Again, ensure you are well-stocked with those vital contact lens fluids and solutions.

Health

There are no mandatory vaccination requirements. However, you may be advised by your doctor to take certain precautions. In recent years the US Consulate in Hong Kong has recommended inoculations against hepatitis A and B, Japanese encephalitis B, tetanus, polio, cholera and malaria. The risk of contracting any of these diseases is small, although it increases during the summer months and in rural areas. To minimize risks, remember to only drink mineral or boiled water (supplied in hotels), make sure food is freshly cooked, peel all fruit and avoid raw leafy vegetables.

Bring any prescription medicines you know you will need, and anything you take regularly for your general health. Some of these drugs are available in China, but it is safer if you plan to be self-sufficient. On arrival in China, travellers are required to complete a simple health declaration. Many hotel clinics can deal with minor illnesses and Shanghai has excellent hospitals, with foreigners' sections, for more serious ailments. As far as health insurance is concerned: it is better to be safe than sorry.

A change in regulations in 1993 has allowed foreign doctors to work in China. Following this many joint ventures employing foreign staff have been established in Shanghai. These include the Ruijin Hospital, 197 Ruijin Lu (tel. 433-3725); the Huadong Hospital, 221 Yanan Xi Lu (tel. 240-3180); and the Shanghai First People's Hospital, 585 Jiulong Lu (tel. 306-9478). Excellent dental treatment is available at the Post and Communication Dental Clinic at 666 Changle Lu (tel. 247-4215). There is an Emergency Centre at 68 Haining Lu (tel. 324-4010) and a branch of International SOS Assistance at 2004 Nanjing Xi Lu (tel. 248-3040).

Climate And Clothing

Shanghai experiences extremes of climate. Winters are cold with occasional snowfalls and lots of rain. Summer is very hot and muggy with daytime highs often reaching

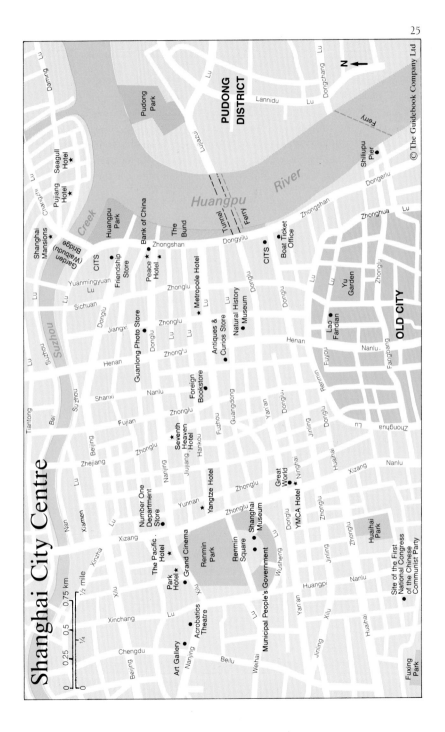

Shanghai City Centre

© The Guidebook Company Ltd

N

PUDONG DISTRICT

Huangpu River

Suzhou Creek

OLD CITY

Garden (Waibudu) Bridge

Shanghai Mansions ★
Seagull Hotel ★
Pujiang Hotel ★

Huangpu Park
Bank of China
The Bund
CITS
Friendship Store
Peace Hotel ★
Metropole Hotel ★
Zhongshan

Pudong Park

Shilupu Pier ★
Boat Ticket Office
CITS ●

Lannidu Lu
Dongchang
Dongchang Lu
Dongerlu
Dongyilu
Tunnel
Ferry

Yuanmingyuan Lu
Sichuan
Donglu
Jiangxi
Henan

Guanlong Photo Store
Zhonglu
Donglu
Zhong'lu

Antiques & Curios Store ●
Natural History Museum ●

Yu Garden
Lao Fandian ●
Nanlu
Fangbang

Shanxi
Nanlu
Foreign Bookstore

Fujian
Zhonglu
Beijing
Zhejiang

Seventh Heaven Hotel ★
Jiujiang
Hankou
Nanjing
Fuzhou

Guangdong
Yan'an

Great World
YMCA Hotel ★
Ninghai

Number One Department Store
Yunnan
Yangtze Hotel

Shanghai Museum ●
Renmin Square
Renmin Park

Nan
Xiamen
Xizang
Xinzha

The Pacific Hotel ★
Grand Cinema ★
Park Hotel ★

Municipal People's Government

Xizang
Huaihai Park

Huangpi

Site of the First National Congress of the Chinese Communist Party ●

Fuxing Park

Art Gallery ●
Acrobatics Theatre
Nanjing
Beilu
Chengdu
Xinchang
Beijing

Xilu
Xiujiang

½ mile
¾ km
0.75
0.5
0.25
0
¼
½
0

Huaihai
Jinling
Xilu
Yan'an
Weihai

the mid-to-upper 30s centigrade (90s fahrenheit), although this is not too uncomfortable thanks to frequent breezes off the river and air-conditioning in most hotels.

In spring, the temperature can fluctuate considerably from one day to the next and, even as the weather gets generally warmer, a cold spell can suddenly descend. Early summer is usually wet; during the rainy season, which normally begins around the second week of June and ends in early August, it can rain for days on end and the damp can be very tiresome. Autumn is by far the best time to visit the city. The average temperature is 24°C (75°F) during the day and 14°C (56°F) at night and the skies are as clear as the industrial haze will permit.

Chinese fashion is generally informal, and slightly conservative, so casual, comfortable clothes and sensible shoes are best for travelling. Although formal dress is rarely required, Chinese and foreign businessmen usually wear suit jackets and ties. Similarly conservative attire would also apply to women on business.

AVERAGE TEMPERATURES IN SHANGHAI

Month	Monthly Average		Average High		Average Low	
	°C	°F	°C	°F	°C	°F
Jan	3.3	37.9	7.8	46.0	0.0	32.0
Feb	4.3	39.7	8.7	47.7	1.0	33.8
Mar	8.3	46.9	13.1	55.6	4.5	40.1
Apr	13.8	56.8	19.1	66.4	9.8	49.6
May	18.9	66.0	24.3	75.7	14.9	58.8
Jun	23.2	73.8	28.1	82.6	19.7	67.5
Jul	27.4	81.3	32.3	90.1	24.0	75.2
Aug	27.5	81.4	32.5	90.5	24.0	75.2
Sep	23.2	73.8	28.2	82.8	19.8	67.6
Oct	17.7	63.9	23.2	73.8	13.7	56.7
Nov	11.7	53.1	17.0	62.6	7.7	45.9
Dec	5.9	42.6	10.9	51.6	2.1	35.8

Getting Around Shanghai

Shanghai is a colossal city, but the fairly regular pattern of the main streets crossing at right angles, together with the variety of landmarks, makes it a relatively easy city to get around. Zhongshan Dong Lu, or the Bund as it used to be called, and Nanjing

Lu, where many of the most popular shops and restaurants can be found, will be easily remembered focal points for any visitor to Shanghai, however short the stay. But the crowds take some getting used to; making one's way through the densely packed Nanjing Lu, the Shanghainese say, requires real skill.

In the last few years, traffic jams have become endemic. Thus it is essential to leave plenty of time when making a trip by bus or taxi, particularly at rush hour. Particular bottlenecks, especially as construction work proceeds, are around the major shopping areas of Nanjing Lu and Huaihai Lu. A trip from the Bund to the airport can take 30 minutes at night but well over one hour during the day. This system should gradually ease as the city's major infrastructure projects proceed. Already a new inner ring road has opened and numerous elevated highways are under construction. A staggering total of 1.25 billion US dollars was spent in 1993 and 1994 on improvements to the city's transportation network.

Access to the Pudong New Area, across the Huangpu River, has been facilitated by the construction of the Nanpu and Yangpu bridges as well as two tunnels. Work on another tunnel near Yanan Xi Lu commenced in late 1994. Future plans include two tunnels with moving escalators for pedestrian traffic.

All visitors should be armed with a reasonable map of Shanghai. *The Shanghai Official Tourist Map* is available at no cost at most tourist hotels and is updated quarterly. There is also a pull-out map in the tourist publication *Welcome to China, Shanghai*—again free at most hotels.

Hailing A Taxi

Hailing a taxi in the street is relatively easy—in fact the over-abundance of taxis has forced the Shanghai government into strictly controlling the number of new taxis coming into service. Shanghai taxis are fairly cheap, generally 1.60Rmb per kilometre with a flagfall of 10.80Rmb, and reliable. An additional fee is payable if crossing the Pudong via tunnel.

Receipts are given for every ride, and there is a telephone number for complaints. It is said that a single telephone call from a passenger—regardless of the complaint—can cause a driver to lose his or her job. There are thousands of drivers waiting in line to take over. Taxis can be booked by telephoning 258-0000. A fee of 2 *yuan* is charged for telephone bookings. If you can't speak Chinese, you might pick up a hotel namecard, or get your destination written in characters.

Most hotels have their own taxi fleets or cars that can be booked in advance for day trips, or airport transfers. However, even with a confirmed reservation there can be a long wait due to the difficulty in getting *anywhere* on time in bustling Shanghai, and because a hotel driver may decide to pick up a casual fare while heading back to base. Therefore it is important to stipulate that the car can be on time—or earlier.

The bicycle is still the most efficient form of transport in Shanghai

By City Bus

Shanghai's buses offer convenient, cheap services throughout the city but they are desperately overloaded and at peak hours even a Chinese-speaking visitor should be wary about boarding one. It is also sometimes difficult to locate the appropriate bus stop. However for those wishing a novel Shanghai experience, jump on one up the Nanjing Lu for a short mystery tour around this fascinating city.

Though Shanghai is a relatively safe city be aware of pickpockets, especially in crowded tourist areas. It is best to leave your valuables in a safe deposit box at your hotel. (*One word of advice*: don't forget to carry toilet tissue with you as supplies aren't guaranteed at some local toilets. Also keep a supply of one *jiao* notes or coins for paying entrance fees to some 'up-graded' toilets.)

By Bicycle

The bicycle is still the most efficient form of transport in Shanghai. Some hotels have reasonable hire facilities. Many major roads are forbidden to cyclists before 8 pm, though many roads are likewise forbidden to heavy traffic.

By Metro

The city's first metro line, Number One, should be fully in operation by May 1995. The 16.1 kilometre line with 13 stations runs from the Jiujiang Amusement Park in the south to the Railway Station in the north. It links the fast growing commercial and tourist areas around Xujiahui and Chang Shu Lu with the downtown areas. Rides cost just 1 *yuan*.

Construction of Metro Line Number Two is planned to start in 1995. It will run for 27 kilometres from Hongqiao Airport to Pudong and take four years to complete. There are also plans for the construction of a third metro line.

Entertainment

Shanghai has been an important artistic hub for well over a century now and, though there have been major changes in political and social outlook, the city's cultural output is now richer than at any time since the Communist victory back in 1949. Shanghai is now the cultural and entertainment capital of China, with an exciting array of nightly entertainment ranging from classical and jazz concerts to state-of-the -art, pulsating techno discos. All forms of art (and artists) suffered during the Cultural Revolution, but since the late 1970s, theatres, cinemas, exhibition and con- cert halls have all taken on a new lease of life.

The most important new venue on the cultural scene is the **Shanghai Centre**

Theatre at 1376 Nanjing Xi Lu (tel. 279-8600), a contemporary 1001-seat, multi-purpose theatre fully equipped for drama, opera, ballet, orchestra concerts and films. The spectacular joint-venture office, residential, hotel and commercial complex rises up like Atlantis in the middle of the city. The theatre has revolutionized concert-going in Shanghai by insisting that local audiences follow such Western concert-hall etiquette as not clapping between symphony movements and not entering the hall during performances.

The theatre hosts international performances which range from a top Russian jazz band to the Vienna Boys Choir in 1994, as well as local opera troupes, orchestras and entertainers. Classical mime and Western music in general is undergoing a massive revival in Shanghai. The Shanghai Symphony Orchestra, regarded as the best in the country, gives frequent concerts at the **Shanghai Concert Hall** at 523 Yanan Dong Lu (tel. 327-4383/327-7249); as do the Shanghai Philharmonic Orchestra and also the Shanghai Ballet Troupe. Other concert venues include the **Shanghai Municipal Theatre** at 210 Fuzhou Lu, and the **Renmin Grand Theatre** at 663 Jinjiang Lu (tel. 322-4509). The Jinjiang Hotel also hosts a weekly Chamber Music Concert, each Friday at 8 pm (admission 20 *yuan*). Recitals are also often given at the Shanghai Conservatory of Music.

Foreign tourists in Shanghai tend to see only the shows that CITS select for them. But there are plenty of performances that the adventurous visitor can go to on by themselves. Although a knowledge of some Chinese is an obvious advantage, there is much that can be enjoyed without it. (Besides, it is always possible to just meet some friendly soul who maybe interested in practising their English, or just wants to meet someone with whom to discuss world affairs or exchange stories, and who probably has something of significance or interest to impart.)

Wenhuibao and the *Shanghai Evening News*, two of the local Chinese newspapers, always carry listings of what is on (though in Chinese), as does the *Shanghai Star* (in English). Tickets for shows can be bought through CITS, or you can go directly to the theatre to buy them. Tickets for most shows sell quickly, so if possible get them well in advance of the performance.

Shanghai has 40 specialist companies and some 15 significant professional performing groups in everything ranging from opera, ballet and music to comedy and acrobatics. For a real cultural thrill and dazzling spectacle of sound, movement and colour, one should attend a Beijing—or other local Chinese—opera if one is in town. In listening to Chinese opera the foreign ear must first get acquainted with the use of the voice in high falsetto before the richness of melodic invention, the drama of the music and the rigorous artistry of the performers can be appreciated. (Chen Kaige's brilliant film *Farewell My Concubine* is a splendid—and highly dramatic—portrayal of the turbulent lives of two performers of this richly artistic discipline.)

THE FLOWERS ON THE SEA

A 19th-century novel by Han Bangqing, The Singsong Girls of Shanghai, begins with a prologue in which the author dreams he is walking on a sea bobbing with flowers. The meaning of this will not be lost on the average Chinese reader, for Shanghai translates as Above-the-Sea and 'flower' is a euphemism for a prostitute.

Prostitution was one of Shanghai's established institutions. The singsong houses (some of which remain standing in Shantou Lu and Fuzhou Lu, though long turned to other uses) had names like the House of Sure Satisfaction and the Hall of Beauties inscribed in red on the glass lanterns outside their doors. The high-class ones would have a strip of red paper posted on the door with the courtesan's name on it. Stepping inside, the patron found himself in a parlour with little rooms partitioned off it. The sound of music might reach his ears—for the girls were entertainers as well as prostitutes—as servant girls appeared to welcome him with tea and bowls of nuts and sweetmeats. A meal would be laid out, with waiters scurrying to bring the caller bowls of cooked dishes and cups of warmed wine.

Next, a pipe would be offered. Lying on a lacquered divan, the patron would watch as his favourite courtesan heated his opium, rolling the paste into a pellet and roasting it over a flame.

With its maidservants, 'aunties' (madams), drinking parties and regular customers, the Shanghai singsong houses had a domestic feel to them. To call them whorehouses would be to do them a disservice. Some of them were select establishments, frequented only by the well-heeled. The most select were the shuyu, or 'storytellers' residences', so named because many singsong girls had begun their careers as teahouse balladeers.

The higher the grade of a courtesan, the more one paid for her company. Among the most expensive were the qing guanren, the virgin courtesans. They were a kind of apprentice, to deflower whom was the privilege of only the very rich. Summoned to a party or an assignation, these girls made their way through the crush of Shanghai's alleys by riding on the shoulders of their ponces.

Whatever her rank, it was the dream of every singsong girl—who knew only too well how transient were her bloom and beauty—to become the principal wife of her patron. Sadly, the dream seldom came true, for while a man was happy enough to take his favourite singsong girl as a concubine, he demurred at making her his wife.

Colourful cigarette advertisement

Almost everyone who visits Shanghai will go to see a performance by the world famous Shanghai Acrobatic Troupe. The troupe will stun the spectator by its sheer versatility and power. The **Shanghai Acrobatic Theatre** at 400 Nanjing Xi Lu (tel. 327-3573) was China's first modern acrobatics and circus theatre. It has a circular stage, and cages for tigers, monkeys and dogs at the back. Those wishing to see acrobatics without animal performances should try to visit one of the local acrobatic shows—the best being at the Art Deco **Lyceum** (Lan Xin), directly across from the Jiujiang Hotel, which also hosts local dramatic performances, at 57 Maoming Nan Lu (tel. 256-4631).

The major cinemas of Shanghai show a wide variety of Chinese films and, less frequently, foreign films. The foreign films shown on general release (and on television) are usually dubbed, although occasionally they may be subtitled. Tickets are very cheap and if the film is sold out there are always ticket touts operating outside the cinemas who will gladly provide you one—at a price, of course, but cheap all the same. The **Shanghai Film Studio** at Xujiahui can be visited, but you have to apply through CITS. Once the Hollywood of China, Shanghai still has a considerable film industry, though the most original films in recent years have come out of studios elsewhere (such as Xi'an). The cinema has played no small part in China's recent history, and in the 1930s the film companies in Shanghai were among the places most deeply infiltrated by the Communists. Besides, if a certain starlet called Lan Ping, one day to be so famous as Jiang Ching, had been more successful in Shanghai, she might not have taken off for the Communist base in Yanan and caught the eye of Mao Zedong. And there is no knowing what might have happened to China if there had been no Madame Mao to urge it towards ever loftier revolutionary heights. Even as China's First Lady, she remained starry-eyed about Hollywood, which was a part of the dream she had once had in Shanghai, where, as an unknown, she had sat spellbound through *Camille*, *Queen Christina* and other Greta Garbo classics.

Three of the larger pre-liberation cinemas are the **Meiqi** (Majestic) **Theatre**, 66 Jiangning Lu (tel. 217-4409), **Daguangming** (Grand) **Cinema**, 216 Nanjing Xi Lu (tel. 327-4260), and **Guotai** (Cathay) **Theatre**, 870 Huaihai Zhong Lu (tel. 437-2592). **The Shanghai Film Art Centre** next to the Holiday Inn on Xin Hua Lu (tel. 240-0668) has five international standard movie theatres, besides one of the biggest discos in Shanghai. (As from December 1994, smoking has been banned from all theatres, cinemas and concert halls.)

A regular fixture on the Shanghai nightlife scene is the wheezy but tenacious jazz band that plays in the lounge of the Peace Hotel from 8 pm—11 pm. The musicians, all advanced in years, had to practise in secret during the Cultural Revolution—or so the story goes. There is a cover charge and drinks are relatively expensive, though an evening spent in the Tudor-style bar nostalgically dancing away or toe-tapping is an unforgettable experience, and an imaginative glimpse into the heady bygone days of pre-revolutionary, hedonistic Shanghai nightlife. Get there early—the jazz band is a real crowd-puller.

Certain aspects of the lifestyle that lent Shanghai the sobriquet 'Paris of the East' in the 1930s are gradually being revived in the 1990s. Nowhere is this more evident than in Shanghai's nightspots, where the clientele is mostly local and foreign businessmen, many from Hong Kong and Taiwan, who bring along their girlfriends or secretaries—and their portable telephones—although one also finds a smattering of die-hard foreign tourists, or foreign students escaping the restricted atmosphere of their Chinese university campus in search of Shanghai's elusive Dionysian reputation.

Shanghai nightlife centres around three types of venues: the hotel discos, karaoke (literally meaning in Japanese 'empty orchestra') and bars; the joint-venture nightclubs; and the privately run bars. As one would expect, fashions in bars and discos change fast, and some of the smaller bars are as short-lived as butterflies, but each memorable in their own way.

The better-known discos are the **Reading Room** in the JC Mandarin; the **Passion Disco** in the Galaxy Hotel, a joint venture with a Taiwanese entrepreneur where the logo resembles Madonna's lips and the disc jockey is from Singapore; **Nicole's** at the Sheraton Hua Ting; the **Casablanca** at the Hongqiao Hotel; **The Talk of the Town** at the Hotel Equatorial; and the **Starlight** at the Yangtze New World. **JJ Disco** at 1127 Yanan Zhong Lu, near the Hilton, is China's biggest and brashest disco hot spot.

For music to listen and drink to rather than dance, the Hilton's **Penthouse Bar and Lounge** provides a spectacular view of the city and an Australian duo, while the 24 hour **Shanghai Express** restaurant on the lower ground floor has an American band playing from 10 pm–2 am nightly except Mondays. Filipino musicians steal the show at **Charlie's** in the Holiday Inn Crowne Plaza, the **lobby lounge** at the Sheraton Hua Ting, and **Trader's Pub** at the JC Mandarin. There is always fine music at **Cosmos** in the Lan Sheng Hotel. The **Top Ten** at the Portman Shangri-La features a live band every evening. For those with classical tastes, a pianist and string quartet entertain at the **Bubbling Well Lounge** in the same hotel. The elegant **Oasis Lounge** (Garden Hotel) stands on the site of a former swimming pool used by Mao.

Lovers of karaoke (KTV) can sing to their heart's content and dance at **Wind** in the Galaxy Hotel; at the **Shinko Golden Key Club** on Yanan Lu near the Bund with its fine restaurant and upmarket bar tended by a bevy of beautiful hostesses; and at the **Shanghai Art Club** at 398 Changle Lu, which has a piano bar and restaurant in addition to its very impressive Hop Disco, unique in Shanghai for being smoke-free (though there is an attached smoking room). Other popular Karaoke venues are at the **Yangtze New World Hotel**, the **Sofitel Hyland**, the **New Town Club** and the **Space Dream World** at 222 Cao Xi Lu.

The Shanghai Exhibition Centre

Longhua Pagoda

For a taste of authentic downmarket, low-rent Shanghai nightlife, hop amongst the dozens of small private bars that have sprung up in two constellations: the first in the neighbourhood of the Jinjiang and Garden hotels, and the second near the Hilton and Shanghai hotels. Some foreign businessmen prefer to let their hair down in the intimate atmosphere that makes these small bars appealing and attractive. However, it pays to be a little cautious when setting foot into one of these tiny places for the first time; check the price of drinks before ordering to avoid complicated misunderstandings when paying your bill.

If you fancy having a couple of pints near the Bund area, pop into the **Shanghai Bund Brewage Co.** premises at the side of the old Customs House, 11 Hankou Road. It's Shanghai's first micro-brewery serving its own 'Fest' beer.

Sports And Fitness

Most of the major hotels in Shanghai have extensive sports and exercise facilities for their guests, including swimming pool, steam bath, sauna, gymnasium and massage service. Other features include tennis and squash courts, jacuzzis, billiards rooms and bowling alleys.

The **Shanghai International Golf and Country Club** at Zhu Jia Jiao, Qingpu County (tel. 897-2520) hosts the first golf course in the city for over 40 years. Located 50 kilometres (30 miles) west of the city centre, this Sino-Japanese-US venture has an 18 hole par 72 Championship course designed by Robert Trent Jones. The club also offers six all-weather and lawn tennis courts, a swimming pool and a panoramic cycling path. The clubhouse, built in '19th-century British colonial' style, features a Japanese restaurant, sauna, pro shop and bar. This is a members only club, with entrance fees running from around US$30,000 for individuals to US$100,000 for corporations. However, short-term visitors to Shanghai staying at the Westin, Garden and Airport hotels, as well as members' guests, can make use of those hotels' corporate membership privileges.

For those staying in the Hongqiao Development Zone, the **New Town Club** at 35 Loushangua Lu (tel. 275-7888) has squash and tennis courts, bowling alleys, a gymnasium, sauna, steam bath and several games rooms. The **Shanghai International Club** (tel. 279-1688) offers similar facilities plus an Olympic size indoor swimming pool, jacuzzis and an exclusive lounge with its own library. It is situated in the Shanghai Hotel Equatorial and is open to subscribing members and hotel guests. Tennis courts are available at 1038 Long Huashan Lu (tel. 252-4436) and the **Fuxing Tennis Club** at 1380 Fuxing Zhong Lu (tel. 431-1846).

Church And Worship

Anyone interested in discovering how many Shanghainese spend their Sunday would find a visit to a church worthwhile. It can be a moving experience to witness the faithful resuming an aspect of their lives which had been so long denied them. It is best to go as early as possible in the morning, around 7.30 am, to get a good seat. Foreigners will always be made very welcome.

Shanghai's large Moslem community, made up mostly of people from China's northwestern province of Xinjiang, has its own mosques. There are no synagogues left in Shanghai and the city's Jewish community, which was quite large before 1949, no longer exists (see page 104).

But the city is full of reminders of the time when it had no fewer than 300 congregations, including Protestant, Roman Catholic, Islamic, Russian Orthodox, Jewish, Buddhist and Japanese Shinto. One of these, a beautiful Russian Orthodox church, is worth a visit even though it is now used as a warehouse. It is on Xinle Lu, a couple of blocks from the Jinjiang Club. Go down Changle Lu, and turn left by the Red House Restaurant. Then walk two blocks to Xinle Lu and turn left. The church is about half way down the street.

■ **International Church**: This Protestant church at 53 Hengshan Lu is also known today by its old name, Community Church. Built in 1925, it is perhaps the church best known to foreigners. Sunday services are at 7.30 am and 10 am.

■ **Kunshan Protestant Church**: On Kunshan Lu, this delightful church was reopened in late 1981. Sunday services are at 7.30 am and 9.30 am. There is also a regular evening service.

■ **Xujiahui Cathedral (St Ignatius Cathedral)**: One of Shanghai's most famous landmarks, the Cathedral at 201 Caoxi Bei Lu was reopened in November 1979. There are daily services at 5.30, 6.15 and 7.00 am. There are five services every Sunday morning beginning very early at 4.45 am. The last service commences at 9.30 am. (See also page 56)

■ **Zhabei Church**: This Protestant church, at 8 Baotong Lu, is a 15-minute walk north from the main railway station. It was reopened in July 1982 after being closed for 16 years. The outside is painted a creamy colour which throws the church into stark contrast with the run-down air of the surrounding area. Above the entrance are large red Chinese characters denoting the name of the church, and above the characters hangs a large red cross. Inside there are rows of simple wooden pews with space for some 700 worshippers. A small choir of men and women perform to the accompaniment of a single piano. Services on Sunday are at 7.30 and 9.30 am. There is also

On The Street

I have seen places that were, no doubt, as busy and as thickly populous as the Chinese city in Shanghai, but none that so overwhelmingly impressed me with its business and populousness. In no city, West or East, have I ever had such an impression of dense, rank, richly clotted life. Old Shanghai is Bergson's élan vital in the raw, so to speak, and with the lid off. It is Life itself. Each individual Chinaman has more vitality, you feel, than each individual Indian or European, and the social organism composed of these individuals is therefore more intensely alive than the social organism in India or the West. Or perhaps it is the vitality of the social organism—a vitality accumulated and economized through centuries by ancient habit and tradition. So much life, so carefully canalized, so rapidly and strongly flowing—the spectacle of it inspires something like terror. All this was going on when we were cannibalistic savages. It will still be going on—a little modified, perhaps, by Western science, but not much—long after we in Europe have simply died of fatigue. A thousand years from now the seal-cutters will still be engraving their seals, the ivory workers still sawing and polishing; the tailors will be singing the merits of their cut and cloth, even as they do to-day; the spectacled astrologers will still be conjuring silver out of the pockets of bumpkins and amorous courtesans; there will be a bird market, and eating houses perfumed with delicious cooking, and chemists' shops with bottles full of dried lizards, tigers' whiskers, rhinoceros horns and pickled salamanders; there will be patient jewellers and embroiderers of faultless taste, shops full of marvellous crockery, and furriers who can make elaborate patterns and pictures out of variously coloured fox-skins; and the great black ideographs will still be as perfectly written as they are to-day, or were a thousand years ago, will be thrown on to the red paper with the same apparent recklessness, the same real and assured skill, by a long fine hand as deeply learned in the hieratic gestures of its art as the hand of the man who is writing now. Yes, it will all be there, just as intensely and tenaciously alive as ever—all there a thousand years hence, five thousand, ten. You have only to stroll through old Shanghai to be certain of it. London and Paris offer no such certainty. And even India seems by comparison provisional and precarious.

Aldous Huxley, Jesting Pilate: The Diary of a Journey, 1926

Shanghai has countless food stalls offering an array of local snacks

the occasional evening service. Communion is by invitation only, though foreigners are always made welcome by the pastors who look after the church.

■ **Mu'en (Baptised with Mercy) Church:** In the summer of 1988, some 1,500 Protestants packed this church for the consecration of two bishops, the first to be installed in China in over 30 years. Used as a school until 1979, this former Methodist church can be found in Xizang Zhong Lu between Jiujiang Lu and Hankou Lu.

■ **Xiao Taoyuan Mosque:** Moslems evoking the name of Allah go to the 60-year-old mosque at 52 Xiao Taoyuan Lu. The mosque was built in 1925, and services are at the traditional times of the day for Moslems.

Shopping

For the Chinese, Shanghai is easily the country's finest shopping centre. For the foreign visitor, too, Shanghai's shops are among the best stocked in China.

Mention shopping to any local Chinese, and he will think of Nanjing Lu. Divided into two—Nanjing Dong (East) Lu and Nanjing Xi (West) Lu—this busiest of Shanghai's streets stretches for nearly ten kilometres (six miles), from the Bund to Jiangsu Lu. Lined with cinemas and eating places as well as shops, Nanjing Lu is constantly jammed with pedestrians and crowded buses. Most of these, the locals say, are out-of-towners, country people enriched by the new economic measures . The Shanghainese themselves prefer to shop at Huaihai Lu, the Avenue Joffre of old. Branches of all the established shops can also be found on Jinling Dong Lu, the focus of a municipal attempt at urban renewal which has made a part of this road, lined with colonnaded walkways and fitted with benches for anyone who wants to take the weight off their feet, an interesting area to stroll in.

A new shopping district has also been established in the vicinity of the Xujiahui Cathedral. Furthermore, massive underground shopping cities have been developed around a number of Shanghai's metro stations. The Yu Gardens area has also been transformed, with new outlets added.

Shanghai is experiencing a massive retail revolution which has not only resulted in the upgrading of existing stores, but also the development of ultra-modern joint-venture stores which can rival those in the West. In fact the Nanjing and Huaihai Roads are becoming similar to the main shopping streets of any Western capital city.

Similarly the Huaihai Lu is fast regaining its former 'Avenue Joffre' reputation for luxury and is attracting considerable foreign investment: 24 projects were under construction in early 1995, confirming the district governments intention to emulate Tsim Sha Tsui in Kowloon, Hong Kong. The main shopping streets already surpass Hong Kong in terms of flood-lighting with neon lights and illuminated advertisements on gigantic electronic screens extending 'daylight' and potential shopping hours.

There has been a trend towards restructuring the city's state stores, which now have to compete in a market environment—which has resulted in food outlets, bars and entertainment facilities being added, as well as improved efficiency and service standards. Shareholders, and managers previously denied the ability to act under the centrally planned economy are now able to make smart business decisions.

In the 40 years before 1990, Shanghai's trading and shopping space increased at a rate of nearly 10,000 square metres a year. Over the last three years it has grown by more than one million square metres a year. Nearly 70% of the 150,000 sales businesses in Shanghai are now in private hands. Foreign retailers had invested some US$2 billion in Shanghai retail outlets by the end of 1994.

For most of the local population the new stores are great spectacles offering a new form of evening entertainment—especially as many of the luxury goods are valued at huge multiples of the average salary. For the foreign visitor the shopping revolution has greatly increased availability of certain imported goods, for instance alcohol and toiletries—but the top end of Shanghai stores are much more expensive than those at home. Still Shanghai is a shoppers Nirvana, with many bargains to be found for the gift and souvenir devotees.

DEPARTMENT STORES

Nanjing Lu will remain as China's premier commercial street and the first and foremost department store in Shanghai is, quite literally, the **Number One Department Store** on the corner of Nanjing Dong Lu and Xizang Zhong Lu. Crowded with people and goods, the store serves some 150,000 shoppers each day, and more on holidays. If one has any doubts about Shanghai being the commercial centre of China, a brief look around the Number One Department Store should resolve them once and for all. In 1993 the store's turnover was US$229 million.

The six level store is crammed with high quality domestic goods and some imported ones. It is open until 10 pm and has a money exchange desk.

Also on Nanjing Lu is Shanghai's second largest domestically managed department store, the **Hualian Department Store**. Formerly the Number 10 Department Store it has been spruced up; its colonial features having been altered by gold-tinted glass cladding above its main entrance. Over US$24 million was spent on renovating and enlarging the store in 1994. The store is open until 10 pm.

The newest and most impressive shopping complex is the eight storey **Manhattan Plaza**, located near the Hotel Sofitel Hyland. The building boasts Asia's most modern video screen outside and some of the most up-market shops inside; including Hong Kong designer fashion, jewellery, cosmetics and children's clothing. The complex also has Chinese restaurants, a coffee shop and a kids' play area. Open until 10 pm.

Fallen Angels

He always looked forward to the evening drives through the centre of Shanghai, this electric and lurid city more exciting than any other in the world. As they reached the Bubbling Well Road he pressed his face to the windshield and gazed at the pavements lined with night-clubs and gambling dens, crowded with bar-girls and gangsters and rich beggars with their bodyguards. Crowds of gamblers pushed their way into the jai alai stadiums, blocking the traffic in the Bubbling Well Road. An armoured police van with two Thompson guns mounted in a steel turret above the driver swung in front of the Packard and cleared the pavement. A party of young Chinese women in sequined dresses tripped over a child's coffin decked with paper flowers. Arms linked together, they lurched against the radiator grille of the Packard and swayed past Jim's window, slapping the windshield with their small hands and screaming obscenities. Nearby, along the windows of the Sun Sun department store in the Nanking Road, a party of young European Jews were fighting in and out of the strolling crowds with a gang of older German boys in the swastika armbands of the Graf Zeppelin Club. Chased by the police sirens, they ran through the entrance of the Cathay Theatre, the world's largest cinema, where a crowd of Chinese shopgirls and typists, beggars and pickpockets spilled into the street to watch people arriving for the evening performance. As they stepped from their limousines the women steered their long skirts through the honour guard of fifty hunchbacks in mediaeval costume. Three months earlier, when his parents had taken Jim to the première of The Hunchback of Notre Dame, there had been two hundred hunchbacks, recruited by the management of the theatre from every back alley in Shanghai. As always, the spectacle outside the theatre far exceeded anything shown on its screen.

J G Ballard, *Empire of the Sun*

The perennial rush of Nanjing Lu, with the Oriental Pearl TV Tower in the distance

The established Hong Kong based **Sincere Department Store** has made a return to Shanghai, with six-storey new premises on the Nanjing Xi Lu. Featuring a large variety of imported products, the store is open until 10 pm. Further west on the Nanjing Xi Lu is the **Wings Department Store** with many up-market brands. All goods are either imported or made in Chinese joint-venture factories. There are money changing facilities and international credit cards are accepted. Closing time is 10 pm. The **Landmark Shanghai**, a huge shopping complex under construction on the same street, should be open by mid-1996.

On the Huaihai Zhong Lu are the three new joint-venture stores: The **Maison Mode** boasts Shanghai's first modern Elizabeth Arden Beauty Salon, top fashion designer labels and a coffee shop to rest after the big spend. The Japanese-managed **Isetan Department Store** includes an ice-cream parlour, a bakery, coffee shop, pharmacy and beauty salon. The **Shui Hing Department Store**, which is Hong Kong-managed, features a wide range of imported electrical items.

The Xujiahui district is destined to become a major shopping and commercial centre with developments planned to the year 2000. At the Xujiahui Commercial Plaza, which is accessible by metro (Xuhuihui Station) can be found the **Tai Ping Yang Department Store** and the **Shanghai Oriental Shopping Centre**. The former is a Taiwanese joint-venture with eight floors of shopping and services, which include restaurants, an amusement centre and a crèche. The latter is a Hong Kong joint-venture with four floors of shopping, a 24 hour restaurant, a night club and a pianist in the marble-clad atrium entrance. Nearby are the **Sunrise** and **Pacific** department stores.

Near the Shanghai Hilton at 400 Changle Lu can be found the **Jinjiang Dickson Center**, a Hong Kong joint-venture, where the best international brands and designer labels vie for attention. Charles Jourdan, Guy Laroche and Ralph Lauren are all star names here.

The **Shanghai Centre** was the first and largest multi-use commercial centre in the city, built at a cost of US$195 million by Japanese and US interests. It contains a hotel, apartments, offices, an exhibition hall, a theatre, and a variety of retail outlets that have the makings of an international shopping centre. These include a Wellcome supermarket (Hong Kong style), Watson's (Hong Kong chemist), a Kintetsu department store, as well as bookshops, shops selling jewellery, antiques, rugs and furniture, Chinese medicine shops and restaurants.

The **Shanghai Friendship Store** at 40 Beijing Lu was closed throughout 1994, almost undergoing a total reconstruction. The refurbished six level store will be open in 1995, offering a vast line-up of items ranging from food and drink, clothing, leather goods, arts and crafts treasures to furniture and antiques. A recreation area is planned for the top floor.

The Hongkong and Shanghai Bank Building and interior, completed in 1923

Antiques

No trip to China is complete without a foray into the world of the old Middle Kingdom: in other words, Shanghai's burgeoning antiques markets.

The two principal markets are the daily, permanent market in **Dongtai Lu**, off Xizang Nan Lu, and the Sunday market in **Fuyou Lu**, near the Yu Garden and the Temple of the City God. For those who are experiencing a Chinese antiques market for the first time, Dongtai Lu is an eye-opener. But if you are familiar with Dongtai Lu, the Sunday Fuyou Lu market is, well, something of a foretaste of paradise.

Fuyou Lu features a traditional 'ghost market' (*guishi*), as trading begins before sunrise. Many of those who turn up this early are antiques dealers from Dongtai Lu, eager to be present when the traders unpack their wares. Public transport is infrequent at this early hour—its best to book a taxi the night before or rent a bicycle.

There is usually a stunning range of goods on sale: bits and pieces of battered or broken 19th-century furniture; scholar's triple-tiered boxes; carved, painted and gilded wooden bobbins; a selection of Little Red Books; early maps of Shanghai; and, of course, jade and ceramics—but don't expect to find museum-quality pieces. Many of the dealers subscribe to auction catalogues and know more about antiquities than their modest appearance suggests. On the other hand, the patient explorer may discover something worthwhile for a very reasonable price.

Not a single item at Fuyou Lu has a price tag; making it a haggler's heaven—or hell, depending on you. Bargaining is a matter of course here, and thus the best way to clinch a difficult deal is to walk away when you are within five or ten per cent of your target. Begin by offering 25–30% of the first quoted price and, depending on how eager you are to own the piece, allow yourself to be nudged up to paying 50%–60% of that price.

No sales receipts are issued in either of the markets, and particularly large, valuable pieces may be difficult to export. However, 99% of the gewgaws and curios on sale will receive the green light at customs.

The **Fuyou Lu Sunday market** starts to peter out in the middle of the afternoon. It reaches a peak between about 9 am and 11 am. The Dongtai market is open daily from 9 am to 5 pm, though it is best visited after lunch. Another market well worth finding is located in the basement of the Huabao building in the **Yu Garden** (Yu Yuan) area. **The Yu Yuan Antique Market** has around 200 stalls with items running from a few *yuan* for a Mao badge to over US$100,000 for a dinosaur fossil. Antique hunting, just like the stock market, is a confirmed Shanghai craze.

The state-run antiques outlets, where prices are marked (and tend to be high) but not entirely non-negotiable, are also worth visiting. One of the shops of most interest to tourists is the **Shaanxi Old Wares Store** at 557 Yanan Zhong Lu. It is well stocked with antique furniture made of wood, bronze, lacquer and basketware, and also has jewellery and bibelots. The tourist may also like to check out the Shanghai Arts and Crafts Trade Centre at the **Shanghai Exhibition Centre** (1000 Yanan Zhong Lu), which has an enormous range of merchandise on display, including sculpture, tapestry, woollen needlepoint, folk handicrafts, furniture, clothing, fabrics, and metalwork. Customers make their selection from either the display cabinets or the sales counters, and the centre will arrange packing and shipping if necessary.

The **Shanghai Antiques and Curio Store** at 218–226 Guangdong Lu is also worth a look. The shop has been dealing in antiques for a century, but now sells mostly modern arts and crafts. It has a good selection of traditional paintings in the smaller of its two side-by-side shops. If one happens to be in the area, look in on the **Shanghai Arts and Crafts Store** at 190 Nanjing Xi Lu and the **Yuhua Arts and Crafts Store** at 929–935 Huaihai Zhong Lu. The **Chong Shin** (Chuangxin) **Old Arts and Crafts Store** at 1297 Huaihai Lu stocks objects you will not easily find elsewhere, such as Ningbo-style beds (with balustrades and decorated headboards) and mahogany furniture; carved chairs; Chinese chests, trunks and boxes; red-lacquered tubs; flower pots; teapots, and so on.

For porcelain and ceramics you might try the **Shanghai Jingdezhen Porcelain Artware Store** at 1175 Nanjing Xi Lu and the **Guohua Porcelain Shop** at 550 Nanjing Dong Lu.

BOOKSHOPS

For guides, art and picture books, Chinese and Western periodicals and newspapers, try the **Foreign Languages Bookstore** in the Jinjiang Hotel compound, the **Friendship Store** and the book shops in the **Peace Hotel** and **Sheraton Hua Ting**. The latest foreign mass market paperbacks are available in these and other stores.

If time is a not a problem, you may like to browse at the **Foreign Languages Bookstore** at 380 and 390 Fuzhou Lu; this stocks a wide range of periodicals and books in French, German, English and Spanish. For those who read Chinese, the **Shanghai Bookstore** at 401–11 Fuzhou Lu, the **China Classics Bookstore** at 424 Fuzhou Lu and the **Xinhua Bookstore** at 345 Nanjing Dong Lu are worth a look. If you want to browse, it is best to go early on in the day because the stores get busy very quickly. Even if you don't read Chinese there are papercuts, paintings, bookmarks, rubbings and postcards to look at.

For stamp collectors, the **Shanghai Stamps Company** at 244 Nanjing Dong Lu (open 8.30 am–6 pm) has a reasonable, though not always complete, selection.

SPECIALITY STORES

The place to go for speciality stores is the Old Town, where the **Yu Garden Bazaar** winds through a maze of interesting streets and alleys crammed with little shops as well as larger, newly completed emporiums whose architectural faces have been adopted from the Ming and Qing dynasties. The thrill of shopping in this area is increasing by the day as plans for its development in faithful style are realised. The bazaar is a descendant of the temple fair, the stalls and booths that used to line the approach to the Temple of the Town God (see page 57). It is best to wander around by yourself, if you are not subject to claustrophobia—the bazaar receives over 400,000 customers a day, and double to triple that number on holidays. The language barrier shouldn't be too much of a problem: just point and you will be served. You will find a shop selling just chopsticks; a shop selling umbrellas; a paper pattern store; a lamp and lantern store, a musical instruments store, numerous handicraft stores, food outlets and stores selling incense and temple worship paraphernalia.

One of the best known of the small shops in the bazaar is the **Wanli Walking Stick Shop**, where you may choose between sticks made of wood, bamboo, rattan, willow or metal from various parts of China. If the length is not right for the height of the customer, the shop can adjust it, and also repair the stick if it gets broken.

One of the nicest shops in Shanghai is the **Tiehuaxuan Pottery Shop**, which specializes in the famous violet-sand pottery from Yixing, a town in Jiangsu Province. The pots come in all shapes and sizes, and will make attractive presents to take home. While you are at it, you may also like to buy some of the flowery tea mugs that the shop sells; they come with lids and are a great bargain. Other interesting and inexpensive buys at the bazaar include children's clothes, vegetable carving sets in zipped wallets, bone *mahjong* sets and intricate papercuts. It is expected that the Fumin Commercial Building will be completed in 1996—providing a paradise for shoppers as over 2000 independent traders will set up stalls inside.

Other speciality shops in Shanghai include the following: the **Wang San Kee** (Wang Xinji) **Fan Shop** at 782 Nanjing Dong Lu; the **Zhang Xiaoquan Scissors Shop** at 40 Nanjing Dong Lu. The **Shanghai Arts and Crafts Jewellery and Jade Ware Store**, at 438 Nanjing Dong Lu, has a foreigners' reception area.

OTHER SHOPS

For photographic supplies including film and accessories you can try the **Guan Long**, located at 190 Nanjing Dong Lu.

Shanghai is full of pharmacies selling both Western and Chinese medicines. At the Chinese medicine shops, some of which stretch back to the 19th century, you can buy exotic tonics such as ginseng, pilose antler and Tiger-bone wine (a tonic wine soaked with tiger's bone and papaya). Many of these remedies are from time-honoured recipes passed down through the generations. Those interested in holistic and alternative medicine will find these shops and their natural remedies quite fascinating. Here are a couple of the most famous: the **Cai Tongde** at 320 Nanjing Dong Lu and the **Lei Yunshang** at 719 Nanjing Xi Lu.

Signs of greater spending power in the new age of consumerism

Sights In Shanghai

There are few sights such as the Forbidden City or Temple of Heaven in Shanghai, but the city has something to offer every tourist in the way of sights. Shanghai on a rainy day can have a drab and grey demeanour, but all over the city there are relics of more jazzy times. Walking about its streets, one easily stumbles on architectural survivors of the time when its Western builders considered the city their own.

For the present-day European visitor, Shanghai is a surprising city, for unlike all other Chinese cities it seems unexpectedly like home. Architecturally speaking it is the least 'Chinese' of China's cities. There it sprawls, a medley of British, French, Russian, Japanese and Chinese styles.

The revitalization of the city under the new economic policies and the return of the foreigner through the 'open door' now pose a greater threat to the old buildings than three decades of Communist rule. Understandably, many tourists prefer new, international-style hotels to the ones resurrected from the 1930s. The Garden Hotel offers a fine example of historical preservation, in which a spanking new hotel block was mounted atop the old Jinjiang Club, formerly the Cercle Sportif Français. The hotel is worth a visit if only to take a peek at the Grand Ballroom, with its magnificent stained glass ceiling lamp in the form of a ship's keel. The floating panels in the wooden floor have only been demobilized, not removed.

A visit to the Peace Hotel—formerly the Cathay Hotel, and home to Sir Victor Sassoon's Far Eastern Empire and host to the rich and famous—is an essential part of any sightseeing itinerary. Located on the Bund, the decor and mood of the hotel are highly evocative of the ambience of Thirties Shanghai (see page 121).

European Relics

The Bund (Waitan)

Shanghai is bounded on the east by the Huangpu River, a tributary of which, the Suzhou Creek, crosses it from east to west. A wide avenue curves along the western bank of the Huangpu, dominated on one side by an imposing line of buildings in the grand European style. This impressive avenue, now called Zhongshan Dong Yi Lu, was the famous Bund, probably the best-known of all streets in the East.

Called *Waitan* by the Chinese, the Bund began life as a muddy towpath. Later it became the focal point of the city. It was both a hectic waterfront, with every conceivable kind of boat from sampans to large cargo vessels anchoring there, and, at the same time, one of Shanghai's main streets. Contemporary accounts describe vividly the continuous noisy street activity, as beggars, hawkers and black marketeers mingled with coolies, seamen and the businessmen from the great trading houses and banks that lined the street. The road was constantly jammed with trucks, mule carts, trams, motor cars and rickshaws.

Today Shanghai's main wharves are further downriver, the frenetic street life has gone, and the Bund has acquired a different mood. The road running along the Bund is still as busy as ever—and is now a vital link in the city's new highway network. Pedestrians are now forced underground through subways to emerge on a new elevated walkway along the waterfront.

As one of the city governments key projects for the 1990s, on which work is still continuing, the level of the promenade on the Bund has been raised to prevent possible flooding. Like Venice, Shanghai is slowly sinking. The imperative of raising the Bund has resulted in a wide, well-trodden path for visitors and pleasure-seekers, picture-snapping or relaxing in front of the busy harbour. On the site of the former, very 'British' style Public Gardens, where the Huangpu River converges with Suzhou Creek, now stands a granite monument to the people's heroes.

Against the modern aspect of the Bund, the old buildings sit much as they did 60 years ago, though they are now magnificently illuminated some nights. Though the Bund has undergone a great physical transformation in recent years, it is the up-coming revolution in the economic and social life of the area which will prove to be of perdurable importance. There are plans in the pipe-line to transform it back into the Wall Street of Asia.

Of all the buildings on the Bund, up to early 1995, only a few—including the Customs House and the Peace Hotel—have managed to maintain their former functions. The rest have been occupied by state corporations and government offices. This balance will change as the city plans to lease back 37 of the waterfront buildings to other interested private sector companies. The 220 former tenants have now been approached with a view to reclaiming their properties.

Some banks have already moved back, including ABN AMRO, which has taken up its old premises at the Peace Hotel. The hotel frontage also houses a Citibank lobby with two ATM machines. On the top floor of the hotel, Sir Victor Sassoon's personal suite is to be converted into a bankers' club.

The idea of 'Selling off the Bund' was mooted back in the early 1990s, though little interest was aroused because of the exorbitant prices asked. Since then overseas brokers have been involved in assessing and marketing the properties—each on a 50-year renegotiable lease. However, the process is fraught with difficulties as the state concerns cry for compensation and foreign companies wonder what renovations will be allowed in buildings which appear inefficient in the computer age.

The Bund sell-off symbolises Shanghai's intention to become a major Asian financial capital, though in the long term it is the Pudong New Area which is likely to accede to this prime position.

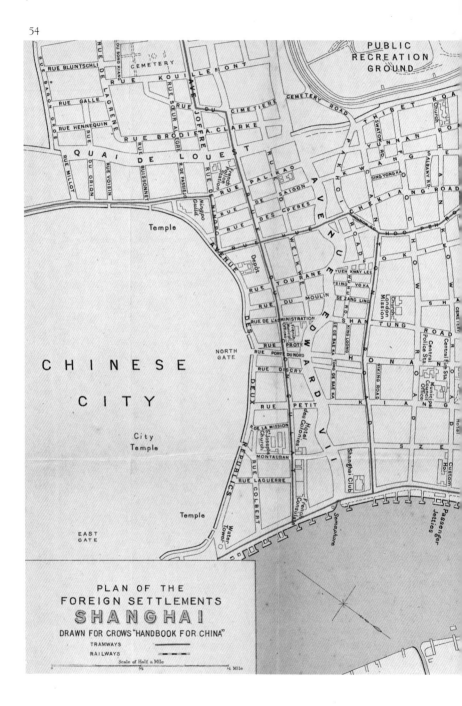

PLAN OF THE
FOREIGN SETTLEMENTS
SHANGHAI
DRAWN FOR CROWS "HANDBOOK FOR CHINA"
TRAMWAYS
RAILWAYS
Scale of Half a Mile

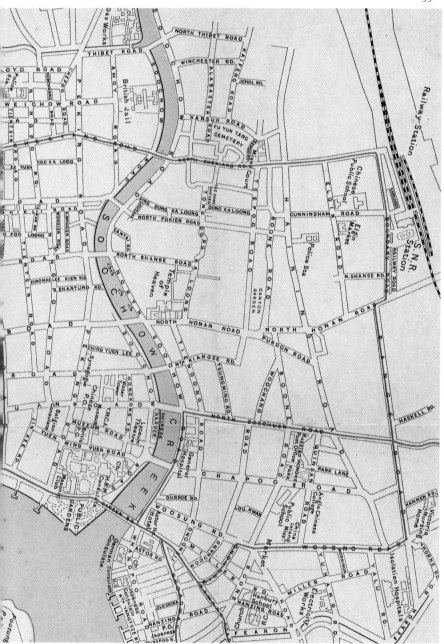

The Foreign Settlements of Shanghai, 1921

■ FORMER OCCUPANTS OF THE BUND

A walk along the Bund is still highly evocative of Shanghai's past. Starting at the
Waibaidu Bridge, which spans the Suzhou Creek (formerly the Garden Bridge), you
pass the gate to the former British Consulate; looking back you see the old Russian
Consulate, still serving the same function. Continuing southwards you will pass the
former buildings of the NYK Line (No. 31), the Banque de L'Indo-Chine (No. 29,
built 1914), the Glen Line (No. 28, 1922) and the Jardine Matheson Company (No.
27, 1922), the Yangtze Insurance Association (No. 26, 1916), the Yokohama Specie
Bank (No. 24, 1924), the Bank of China (No. 23, 1936), the Cathay Hotel (No. 20,
1929); then after crossing the Nanjing Lu, the Palace Hotel (No. 19, 1906), the Char-
tered Bank of India, America and China (No. 18, 1923), Russo-Chinese Bank (No.
15, 1902), Bank of Communications (No. 14), the Customs House (No. 13, 1927),
the Hongkong and Shanghai Bank, now the Shanghai Municipal Government Headquarters (No. 12, 1923); south of the Guangdong Lu is the former Union Building
(No. 4, 1915), the Shanghai Club, now the Dong Feng Hotel (No. 3, 1911) and the
McBain Building (No. 1, 1915).

Xujiahui Cathedral (Xujiahui Dajiaotang)

Located in Xujiahui district in the southwest of the city, the Cathedral of St Ignatius
was built by the Jesuits in 1906. Xujiahui, pronounced and spelt Siccawei (or Ziccawei) in earlier times, has been a Jesuit settlement since the 19th century. The foundation of the complex was laid out in 1848. Jesuit mission work started there because it
was the birthplace of Xu Guangqi, the renowned Chinese pupil of Matteo Ricci.

During the Taiping Rebellion in the middle of the 19th century the area was used
as the headquarters of the rebels. Later it became a prominent missionary centre,
with a meteorological observatory, a college and seminary, an orphanage, an industrial school, a library and publishing house. Xujiahui Cathedral is Shanghai's largest
Catholic church and has room for 2,500 people at any given service although many
more come and have to stand. Its restored bell tower is 49 metres (160 feet) high.

Traditional Chinese Relics

THE OLD TOWN (NANSHI)

Located to the south of Renmin Lu and bordered by Zhonghua Lu, the Chinese Old
Town is the oldest inhabited part of Shanghai. It was here in the 19th century that
international missionary groups set up their first churches and communities. Today

these churches no longer exist and neither do the tightly-packed, rat-infested slums which once occupied the area. Though the streets have now been cleaned up, they are still narrow and crowded, giving the Old Town a special air that hints of past adventure and strange happenings.

The past is being re-invented with vigour as plans to renovate the area around Yu Garden progress. Phase 1 of the project was completed in September 1994, with the erection of eight large new buildings and the renovation of many old stores. Keeping a classical style the new development is increasing the vitality of the area with one edifice, the Huabao Building, having a large area set aside for displaying collections from the city's private museums. Many of the new buildings have been occupied by small independent traders parading an interesting selection of goods and services.

The second phase of development, which began late 1994, encompasses a much larger area of the Old Town and will rely heavily on foreign investment. The area in question will be bounded by Renmin Lu, Henan Nan Lu, Fangbang Zhong Lu and the Bund.

A focal point of the Old Town used to be the Temple of the Town God, Chenghuang Miao. Every Chinese town had one, and it was customary for the temple court to be turned into a veritable fairground on feast days, with traders setting up stalls and entertainers giving performances. The redevelopment will allow the main hall of the temple—which has been a shop for many years—to revert to its more divine business.

HUXINTING TEAHOUSE (HUXINTING CHASHI)
Should you get tired of walking around the Old Town you can always rest in the beautiful old Huxinting (mid-lake) Teahouse. The teahouse stands in the middle of a rectangular pool near the entrance to the Yu Garden, and is supposed—by Europeans—to be the original of the teahouse pictured on 'willow pattern' plates. The Bridge of Nine Turnings (zig-zagged, it is said, because evil spirits cannot turn corners) leads to the old five-sided teahouse pavilion. The teahouse is packed throughout the day with workers and retired people, who come to sip tea, talk, and watch the endless stream of passers-by in the surrounding streets of the old Chinese city. One of Huxinting's most famous visitors in recent times was Britain's Queen Elizabeth II, whose tour of Shanghai included a stop there for a cup of tea. Tea accompanied by snacks (dianxin), such as tasty glutinous rice bound in a banyan leaf parcel, costs around 25 yuan.

YU GARDEN (YU YUAN)
No visit to the Old Town is complete without a tour of the Yu Garden, which lies to the north behind high walls. A fully restored classical Chinese garden, it is similar to

many of the famous gardens of Suzhou. Work on laying out the garden, which was created by a Ming official, Pan Yunduan, for his father, was begun in 1537.

For many Chinese, gardens were a microcosm in which the skilful gardener—who had to combine the qualities of a painter, poet, architect, and sculptor—could construct his own world using minerals, plants and animals in a confined space. Although the Yu Garden occupies less than two hectares (five acres), it seems far larger. The garden demonstrates perfectly the sophisticated art of combining several different elements to create a world in miniature—ingeniously mingling pavilions and corridors, small hills and carefully selected and placed rocks, lotus ponds with goldfish swimming in them, bridges, winding paths, trees and shrubs.

There are many details in the garden to look out for. Each section is divided up by white curving walls that are topped by the undulating body of a dragon. The walls end with splendidly carved dragon heads. There are fine examples of the type of carved bricks found in Suzhou's gardens—earthenware pictures of animals, flowers or scenes illustrating legends. Many shapes and designs of ornamental windows — square, round, rectangular and polygonal—can be seen, with highly complicated lattice-work patterns.

The garden contains over 30 pavilions, and a labyrinth of stairs, corridors and pathways. A large, curiously shaped rock, standing in front of the Hall of Jade Magnificence (Yuhuatang) is known as the Exquisite Jade Rock (Yulinglong) and was, it is claimed, intended for the collection of a Northern Song Dynasty (960–1127) emperor. During the Taiping Rebellion some citizens of Shanghai, known as the 'Society of Little Swords', joined this peasant uprising against the Qing Dynasty, organizing a rebellion from within the walls of the city in 1853. They used the Hall of Heralding Spring (Dianchun Tang) as their headquarters, and managed to inflict considerable damage on foreign and imperial troops before they were finally defeated in 1954. The hall now contains a small museum of the uprising.

Of the restored structures of the garden, Three Ears of Corn Hall (Sansuitang) is the largest. Carved on its doors and windows are rice ears, millet, wheat seedlings, melons and fruit—symbols of plenty. Note the essay on the Yu Garden by its first owner Pan Yunduan, displayed on the wall facing the entrance. Next the visitor comes to the Hall for Viewing the Grand Rockery (Yangshan Tang), which is a beautiful two-storey structure with its balustrade overlooking a pond. Upstairs is the Chamber for Gathering the Rain, which derives its name from a poem by a 17th-century poet containing the line 'Pearl curtains gather the rain from the western mountains in the dusk'.

Over the pond leading to the Grand Rockery (Dajiashan) is the Corridor for Approaching the Best Scenery. The Grand Rockery, built of 2,000 tonnes of yellow stone quarried from Zhejiang Province and cemented together with a kind of rice

Yu Garden

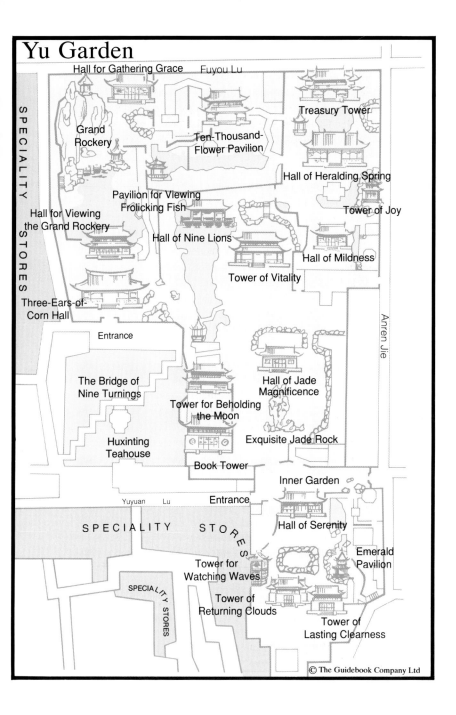

Hall for Gathering Grace

Fuyou Lu

Treasury Tower

Grand Rockery

Ten-Thousand-Flower Pavilion

Hall of Heralding Spring

Pavilion for Viewing Frolicking Fish

Hall for Viewing the Grand Rockery

Tower of Joy

Hall of Nine Lions

Hall of Mildness

Tower of Vitality

Three-Ears-of-Corn Hall

Anren Jie

Entrance

The Bridge of Nine Turnings

Hall of Jade Magnificence

Tower for Beholding the Moon

Huxinting Teahouse

Exquisite Jade Rock

Book Tower

Inner Garden

Yuyuan   Lu

Entrance

Hall of Serenity

SPECIALITY   STORES

Emerald Pavilion

Tower for Watching Waves

SPECIALITY STORES

Tower of Returning Clouds

Tower of Lasting Clearness

SPECIALITY STORES

© The Guidebook Company Ltd

glue, stands 14 metres (46 feet) high in the heart of the garden. At the foot of the rockery, beside a rivulet, is the Pavilion for Viewing Frolicking Fish (Yulexie). Nearby is a 200-year-old wisteria. A gingko tree, said to be 400 years old, stands in front of the Ten Thousand Flower Pavilion (Wanhua Lou). Also worth noting is the Hall of Mildness (Hexu Tang), which contains a century-old set of furniture made of banyan tree roots.

The garden is highly popular with the residents of Shanghai and with Chinese tourists from the rest of the country—particularly the young who come here to photograph each other—and can sometimes be extremely crowded.

TEMPLE OF THE JADE BUDDHA (YUFO SI)

This temple, famous for its two Jade Buddha statues, stands amid the factories and urban sprawl of the northwest of the city. Now in active use, with a number of Buddhist monks in attendance, the temple escaped destruction by the Red Guards because the abbot bolted the doors and plastered them all over with pictures of Chairman Mao—which it would have been a sacrilege to have tampered with. The temple walls and the enormous gilded wooden statues have been repainted in bright colours.

The complex of temple buildings is comparatively new, built in 1911 and 1918, and is curiously misplaced in Shanghai; the temple being characteristic more of those found in distant western China. The Jade Buddhas were brought to Shanghai from Burma in the 1870s. At ground level there is a small graceful reclining Buddha, and, in a special hall reached by climbing up some very steep wooden stairs, there is the larger seated Buddha, with inlaid precious stones decorating the robes. Among other treasured items is a complete set of the Buddhist scriptures printed in 1890. Shoes should be removed before visiting the large Buddha; photography is not permitted.

The Grand Hall building is particularly impressive with twenty heavenly king statues flanking the walls, a huge Sakyamuni image at the front and a magnificent mural sculpture at the back representing Suddhana in search of immortality.

There are polyglot guides on hand who speak several Western languages, and also a restaurant offering interesting vegetarian food. Visitors may also pay for the Buddhist services to be performed at the temple for the souls of their deceased kin. The temple is always crowded with Chinese and foreign tourist groups, and it is wise to visit around 8 am or after 4 pm.

JING'AN TEMPLE (JING'AN SI)

This Buddhist temple dates back to the 19th century and was known to Shanghai's foreign residents as the Bubbling Well Temple. Situated opposite the small, much used Jing'an Park, and just off the busy Nanjing Xi Lu, the temple today belies its Chinese name of the Temple of Tranquillity.

Statuary at the Jade Buddha Temple

The temple's colourful past is probably more interesting than the present buildings, which have recently been restored and are not especially spectacular. Before 1949, it was one of the richest and most constantly used of Shanghai's many temples. It was run by the notorious Abbot of Bubbling Well Road, a massive shaven-headed man, six foot four inches tall, who had a fabulously wealthy wife, seven concubines, and his own White Russian bodyguard.

Longhua Pagoda And Temple (Longhua Ta And Longhua Si)

This attractive eight-sided pagoda in the southwest of the city was first built in AD 274, and then rebuilt in the early Song Dynasty in the tenth century. With seven storeys, the 40 metre (130 foot) high brick and wood structure is a prominent landmark. Under each of the upturned eaves, a little bell hangs. It was a popular tourist spot for foreigners during the first half of this century. That the building tilts slightly to one side gave it added interest.

The temple buildings, which date from the Qing Dynasty (1644–1911), cover a large area. There are five halls with courtyards: the Laughing Buddha Hall, the Hall of the Heavenly King, the Grand Hall, the Three-Sage Hall and the Buddhist Abbot Chamber. As is customary, a bell tower stands to one side of the Grand Hall and a drum tower on the other.

Behind the temple a restaurant serves vegetarian meals and refreshments. The pleasant horticultural gardens nearby are full of attractive seasonal displays of potted plants—rhododendrons, orchids, freesias, azaleas, and miniature *bonsai* landscapes with rocks and flowers.

Chinese sightseers like to visit Longhua in the spring, when the peach trees, for which the park is famous, are in flower. However, a visit over the Chinese New Year will provide the most unforgettable experience as half the population of Shanghai flocks to the Temple fair with hundreds of food stalls and a real buzz of excitement.

Chenxiangge Temple

Reopened in late 1994, Chenxiangge—located near the Yu Garden—is the largest nunnery in the city. The temple was originally the private estate of a Ming Dynasty official, Pan Yunduan, who also owned the Yu Garden itself. The temple was enlarged in the Qing Dynasty (1644–1911), but found itself converted into a factory workshop during the Cultural Revolution when many statues and artifacts were destroyed. Restoration began in 1989 with one master craftsman responsible for recreating the statuary. On the surface of a vault over a gilded statue of Buddha can now be found 348 Buddha figurines representing the 348 Buddhist disciples. Chenxiangge, located at 29 Chenxiangge Lu, is open from 6 am to 4 pm daily.

Studying Buddhist scriptures at the Jade Buddha Temple

The Human Cauldron

The roof garden of the Shanghai Hotel was always crowded at tea-time. Half of it was covered by an awning of the rust-brown colour of Chinese sails, and a large number of tables were under gaily-coloured umbrellas outside the shade of it in a rectangle round a fountain which somewhat cooled the air. The trees and vines in large Chinese oil vessels looked faded, although they were regularly sprinkled with water. Even the floor, tiled with large flat tiles, was wet and gleaming, for it too was sprinkled with water hourly during the summer to temper the heat. Attentive little Chinese waiters hung about the tables with iced drinks and fragrant hot tea for the residents of the British Concession. A string quartet was playing from somewhere unseen in a thin pizzicato which was entirely drowned by the confused burble of talk.

Four American businessmen, shrewd, gray-haired and alert, with their tall highballs in front of them:

"If we get it now it will be more serious than in '32. America can't just fold her arms and look on."

"What the Japanese want is the Monroe Doctrine for Asia. Asia for the Asiatics. Even this they have to copy from us."

"And we'll have the world market flooded with Japanese-dumped goods. And what about all the American capital that's been sunk in China? And what about the oil? If Japan puts China in her pocket who's going to buy our cotton?"

"America's bound to protect her citizens on land and sea, and the Chamber of Commerce will look to it."

"Yes, but we're told that those who do business in foreign countries do so at their own risk."

"The neutrality act—"

"The democratic countries have got to stand together against Japanese Fascism or else go under."

"There's only one thing to do—to make as much money as you can as fast as you can and then beat it for the States."

"That's what we all say, and yet we've been in this infernal hole for thirty years."

"My wife couldn't exist now without six servants."

Two Chinese compradores, one in European dress, the other with an unusually well-cut sleeveless jacket over his long silk robe:

"I always say, better a dog in peace than a man in war."

"The mayor of Peking was bought. He let the Japanese march in without defending the town. He simply opened the city gates."

"It makes no difference. The North was Japanese long ago. It only means the legalization of smuggling through the gap in the North."

"The only question is: can we do better business with the Japanese or against them? Whoever gives me milk is my mother."

"Let us forget these little unpleasantnesses. A man for whom I was able to do an insignificant service has sent me a mandarin fish, and my cook is an artist in cooking it with brown sauce. May I have the pleasure of your company tonight . . ."

Another group, intellectuals, white people, Chinese, a young Siamese, a Norwegian woman with red dyed hair:

"Unless opium is suppressed, China cannot be saved. It is a terrible, ineradicable national vice."

"Like booze in America. Don't forget Prohibition. It only means driving up the price and the consumption."

"Alcohol makes people stupid, and drunkards go home and slaughter their wives. Opium makes you wise and benevolent."

"They say it has an erotic influence."

"Nonsense. It makes you impotent."

"I smoke eight pipes a night, and my hands are steady. You smoke forty cigarettes and your hands shake."

"The anti-opium office does a lot of good. So one hears at least."

"Certainly. They chop the heads off fifty incurables now and again. They give them opium before they do it—to make their death pleasanter."

Four slender and elegant Chinese women under the awning, eating iced fruit:

"Sleeves are going to be worn shorter, my tailor has copied Anna May Wong's."

"Green silk with a bamboo spray of clipped velvet all the way down, at Sincere's sale, a real bargain."

"If my husband brought a concubine into the house I would shoot him."

"The American method. Did you hear Professor Cheifong lecture? It appears that free love is the only system possible for modern people."

"What we need is missionaries for birth-control propaganda."

Two Chinese fanatics sitting over their fine porcelain cups of jasmine tea:

"China is united for the first time. A united China is unconquerable."

"Four hundred million people. We will build walls of our bodies against the Japanese. A beginning has been made."

"We have the people and the patience. In five hundred years China will be the best country in the world. And how short a time is five hundred years!"

"That is so. Ten thousand years of life, my friend!"

"Thank you, honored first-born. Ten thousand years of blessings and contentment!"

The burble of voices, noise and scraps of conversations: they say that Mei Lan Fang has grown old. The New York Stock Exchange has weakened. Whoever wins this war, one thing is certain—we whites can only lose. Better the Japanese than Communists. It is the end of extraterritoriality. What's India going to live on if we cannot export any more opium? Never again shall China be treated as if it were a colony. China—what a hopeless mess! China—what a marvelous country! . . .

Optimists, pessimists, Westerns, Easterns, men, women. Europeans, Americans, Orientals. Courage and cowardice. Idealism and greed. Enmity and love. People of every sort and colour and tendency. Voices, noise, laughter, tristesse, tea, whisky. The full orchestra of every description of humanity: that was teatime on the roof garden of the Shanghai Hotel.

Vicki Baum, Shanghai '37

Revolutionary Relics

SITE OF THE FIRST NATIONAL CONGRESS OF THE CHINESE COMMUNIST PARTY

At 76 Xingye Lu, a small street near Fuxing Park, is a beautifully restored grey brick house where, in July 1921, the Chinese Communist Party was officially born. It was here that the First Party Congress was held. The opening meeting took place at 127 Taichang Lu, but it was here, at the home of one of the founding members on the former Rue Wantz, that the 12 delegates, among them Mao Zedong, held the bulk of their discussions. The meeting was clandestine because it was illegal under the laws of the French Concession. Some days after it started, it was interrupted by a stranger believed to be a spy from the French police. The delegates immediately stopped the meeting and withdrew to Jiaxing County, 113 kilometres (70 miles) south of Shanghai in Zhejiang Province, where they resumed their deliberations on a pleasure boat on Nan Lake.

The room in Xingye Lu where they met is arranged with 12 seats around a table set with tea bowls and ashtrays. In two adjoining rooms is an illustrated history of the Chinese Communist Party, with pictures of a youthful Mao Zedong and other Party founders, a copy of the first Chinese translation of Karl Marx's *Communist Manifesto*, and an account of the lives of the 12 delegates.

SUN YAT-SEN'S FORMER RESIDENCE

Sun Yat-sen, (Sun Zhongshan, 1866–1925), the key figure in the 1911 revolution which brought the Qing, or Manchu Dynasty—and thus the Chinese empire—to an end, is revered by all Chinese, of whatever political colouring, as the founder of modern China. Sun was born into a peasant family living near Macau. At thirteen he was sent to Honolulu; later returning to Guangzhou and Hong Kong to study medicine.

Between 1918 and 1924 he lived at 7 Xiangshan Lu in Shanghai with his wife, Soong Ching-ling. He died in 1925 in Beijing and it was his widow who decided how his memorabilia should be displayed in his old house in Shanghai. There are some evocative photographs, such as the one which shows the couple in front of an aeroplane, the first of its kind to be assembled in China, in Guangzhou. Perhaps the most interesting aspect of a visit is the insight gained through browsing at Dr Sun's 2,700 volume library, with many books in English and other foreign languages. The 'books' are actually photographs of the originals, which have been removed for safe-keeping. Located in a quiet residential area, reminiscent of suburban London or Paris, the house is open to visitors from 9.30 am–11 am and 2 pm–4.30 pm.

SOONG CHING-LING'S FORMER RESIDENCE

The house at 1843 Huaihai Zhong Lu is where Soong Ching-ling, the widow of Dr Sun Yat-sen and honorary president of the People's Republic of China, spent the better part of her life. Dating from the 1920s, the house is set amid evergreen camphor trees in a large and well-tended garden. The house and furnishings are supposedly kept exactly as they were during her lifetime. Her bedroom and office are upstairs. Also upstairs is the bedroom of her devoted maid, Li Yan'e, who worked for Soong Ching-ling for over 50 years. Open from 9 am–11 am and 1 pm–4.30 pm.

Madame Soong, who shortly before her death in 1981 was made an honorary president, was buried next to her parents in the Soong's own burial ground in the Wanguo Cemetery in the suburbs of Shanghai. To one side of her tomb lies that of her maid Li Yan'e's. A well-intentioned but dreadful white marble statue of Madame Soong stands on a granite pedestal in the mausoleum.

ZHOU ENLAI'S FORMER RESIDENCE

In 1946, Zhou Enlai (Chou En-lai) lived at 73 Sinan Lu (Rue Masenet) and headed the Communist Party's Shanghai office there. The house is now a museum, and may be visited by tourists provided an appointment has been made. It was here that Zhou Enlai and his wife Deng Yingchao met and conspired with the rest of the Communist underground in Shanghai. They had to exercise extreme caution because there were always Kuomintang secret agents about. Zhou Enlai was himself a past master of intrigue and espionage, having been an organizer of the Communist secret service in Shanghai. The house is not very home-like, but then it was used as an office and a place for meetings.

LU XUN'S FORMER RESIDENCE, MUSEUM AND TOMB

Lu Xun (1881–1936) was a great man of letters, posthumously hailed as a revolutionary by Chairman Mao. To hear of the revolutionary qualities now attributed to him would probably have surprised Lu Xun, who was a progressive but who never joined the Communist Party. He was an impassioned critic of the Chinese national character, and his famous short story, *A Madman's Diary*, was a repudiation of Confucian culture. While teaching at universities in Hangzhou, Amoy, Canton and Shanghai, he produced essays, poetry, novels (such as his great masterpiece *The True Story of Ah Q*), and many translations of Russian, Japanese and German works. Sometimes referred to as the Chinese Gorky, Lu Xun consistently denounced social injustices.

Lu Xun moved to Shanghai in 1927, where he lived until his death in 1936. He was prominent among the 50 or so intellectuals who first set up the League of Leftist Writers of China in Shanghai in 1930, and who adopted the programme which was to be the charter for the new revolutionary literature in China. Among Lu Xun's

The Cutting Edge

The class struggle remains a living actuality in Shanghai. While I was there an exhibit was on at the Palace of Culture; the theme was the history of the workers' movement: on display were yellowed photographs, newspaper clippings, personal letters alluding to the riots, to the blood-bath repressions. These memories, and a great many more, blaze in the Shanghai worker's mind. It is they who represent Chinese Communism's most extreme left wing: they are impatient of the lingering vestiges of capitalism, are urging the government to shorten the transitional period. There is nothing more farfetched than to suggest, as does Guillain, that Shanghai is a city full of counterrevolutionaries; the mysterious Communist friend who obligingly whispered in his ear that "we've got the backing of only 20 per cent of the population here" sounds like a first cousin of those Western fallen angels several specimens of whom I had the privilege to meet, and whose wishful thinking I was able to judge. No: Shanghai is rather the city where the workers' demands are the most adamantly revolutionary and the most pressing; less well paid than heavy-industry workers, discontent surely does exist among the Shanghai proletariat; but it is just as sure that they have no eagerness to return to the old regime: to the contrary, their complaint is that socialization is not moving ahead fast enough. Contemplate the propaganda posters plastered on walls and decide whether the class struggle is not a heated issue; in Peking, these are fairly mild cartoons: of, for example, a profiteer, green about the gills, staggering under the weight of the sack of money on his back. In Shanghai the pictures are realistic and violent. A soldier has his rifle trained on a counterrevolutionary who, surrounded by an angry crowd, slithers up out of his hiding place in a sewer.

Simone de Beauvoir, *The Long March*

Open Season

The streets were in a ferment of activity. Groups of Red Guards were explaining to clusters of onlookers the meaning and purpose of the Cultural Revolution. Other Red Guards were stopping buses, distributing leaflets, lecturing the passengers, and punishing those whose clothes they disapproved of. Most bicycles had red cards bearing Mao's quotations on the handlebars; riders of the few without them were stopped and given warning. On the sidewalks, the Red Guards led the people to shout slogans. Each group of Red Guards was accompanied by drums and gongs and large reproductions of Mao's portrait mounted on stands. At many street corners, loudspeakers were blaring revolutionary songs at intervals. In my proletarian outfit of old shirt and wide trousers, I blended with the scene and attracted no special attention. I walked steadily in the direction of the bank.

Suddenly I was startled to see the group of Red Guards right in front of me seize a pretty young woman. While one Red Guard held her, another removed her shoes and a third one cut the legs of her slacks open. The Red Guards were shouting, "Why do you wear shoes with pointed toes? Why do you wear slacks with narrow legs?"

"I'm a worker! I'm not a member of the capitalist class! Let me go!" The girl was struggling and protesting.

In the struggle, the Red Guards removed her slacks altogether, much to the amusement of the crowd that had gathered to watch the scene. The onlookers were laughing and jeering. One of the Red Guards slapped the girl's face to stop her from struggling. She sat on the dusty ground and buried her face in her arms. Between sobs she murmured, "I'm not a member of the capitalist class!"

Nien Cheng, *Life and Death in Shanghai*

The Shanghai Underworld

No visitor to pre-1949 Shanghai was likely to miss the underworld life that thronged its streets and alleys. At the lowest end were the professional beggars, organized under beggar kings who took a cut of their takings. Many of them were highly specialized and often highly skilled. Take the Bridge Braves, who 'helped' push carts over the Suzhou Creek and then demanded, as if by right, the fee that their services deserved. Or the 'stationers', who sat on the pavements and invoked the charity of passers-by with persuasively worded and often beautifully handwritten hard-luck petitions. Competition for good sites was keen, and one could not hope to keep one's territory unless one had a protector. Such protectors—or 'uncles' as they were called—were usually gangsters.

Some of Shanghai's most famous underworld personalities were women; viragos who could give as good as they got. Cassia Ma, the Nightsoil Queen, was a celebrated example—nightsoil collection being a lucrative business which the underworld liked to arrogate to itself. For over two decades, it was Cassia, a woman into whose dealings the French gendarmerie would hesitate to inquire too closely, who dominated the trade.

These people depended for their clout on the secret society. The most powerful of the secret societies in Shanghai was the Qing Bang, or Green Gang. The head of it, Big-eared Du (Yuesheng), had followers at every level

greatest legacies to China was a modern style (which he more or less invented) of written Chinese. The creation of a new written language was one of the greatest achievements of the May Fourth Movement of 1919, a cultural renaissance of which Lu Xun was a prominent exponent.

In 1956, Lu Xun's ashes were removed with great ceremony from the international cemetery in the western suburbs to a tomb in the attractive Hongkou Park. In front of the tomb is a bronze statue of the writer. The six characters on the tomb, which say 'Lu Xun's tomb', were inscribed by the late Chairman Mao. The two trees beside the tomb were planted by Zhou Enlai and Lu Xun's widow.

Nearby, in the park, is a museum dedicated to the life and work of the writer. Although many of the exhibits are in Chinese, anyone interested in the history of this era will appreciate the wealth of old newspaper photographs, and others will enjoy the wood block prints illustrating the first editions of Lu Xun's works. There are translations of his works, and of works written on him, as well as reconstructions of his study and bedroom.

of society, from the giants of business to the leaders of beggars. In his time Du Yuesheng had been a fruiterer's assistant, an opium trafficker, a gambling racketeer and a banker. He was also a Kuomintang stalwart, and it was he who helped Chiang Kai-shek put down the Communists in 1927 (in a coup which André Malraux fictionalized in *La Condition Humaine*) and organized the underground resistance work in Shanghai during the Japanese occupation.

Mobsters thrived in Shanghai because there was not just one jurisdiction, but three. And not just criminals, but revolutionaries and conspirators, could make the most of the inconsistencies. The French Concession, where the police could easily be bribed to turn a blind eye, was particularly popular with gangsters and Communists. Indeed, Du Yuesheng's very first partner was Huang Jinrong, the chief detective, and several of his most trusted secret society followers became high-placed Communist officials.

Called the Czar of the French Concession, Du lived in considerable style. Never one to do things by halves, he had five wives in all, two of them famous opera singers. His sons had White Russian bodyguards, and he himself seldom went anywhere without a large entourage. When the Communists came he went to live in Hong Kong. He died there, but was buried in Taiwan. In Shanghai, he remains a household name.

During the last three and a half years of his life before he died of tuberculosis, Lu Xun lived in Shanyin Lu just south of Hongkou Park. The red-brick house is now open to the public, with rooms supposedly arranged in the way they were during Lu Xun's lifetime. The last articles to come from his pen were published in August 1936 and were polemics exposing the Chinese Trotskyite schemes to undermine the Communist party policy of a united national front against Japan. Today he is regarded as being closely linked to the liberation of China's oppressed masses through his satire.

Museums And Exhibitions

SHANGHAI MUSEUM
The Shanghai Museum, which holds one of the finest collections of bronzes, ceramics, painting and sculpture in China, is entering a new phase of its history. Despite a major refurbishment between 1986 and 1991, costing US$1.2 million, the four floors

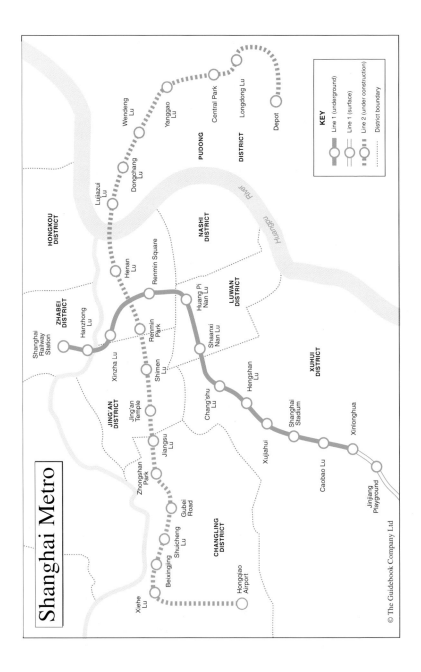

Shanghai Metro

KEY

Line 1 (underground)
Line 1 (surface)
Line 2 (under construction)
District boundary

Huangpu River

PUDONG DISTRICT

Longdong Lu
Depot
Central Park
Yanggao Lu
Wendeng Lu
Dongchang Lu
Lujiazui Lu

HONGKOU DISTRICT

NASHI DISTRICT

LUWAN DISTRICT

ZHABEI DISTRICT

Renmin Square
Henan Lu
Huang Pi Nan Lu
Shaanxi Nan Lu
Hanzhong Lu
Renmin Park
Shanghai Railway Station
Xinzha Lu
Shimen Lu

JING'AN DISTRICT

Jing'an Temple

Hengshan Lu

XUHUI DISTRICT

Chang'shu Lu
Shanghai Stadium
Xinlonghua
Xujiahui
Caobao Lu
Jinjiang Playground

Jiangsu Lu
Zhongshan Park
Gubei Road

CHANGLING DISTRICT

Shuicheng Lu
Beixingling
Xiehe Lu
Hongqiao Airport

© The Guidebook Company Ltd

of display space afforded at the 16 Henan Lu premises—its home since 1952—could not do justice to this important collection. Under 2% of the 120,000 objects—including 15,000 scrolls of painting and calligraphy, and 200,000 books—have actually been on public display in recent times. Thus, in spring 1994 the museum closed and the Art Deco bank building in which it was housed reverted to its former use.

A new museum building, costing US$50 million and part of the massive redevelopment in the People's (Renmin) Square, should be open by late 1995. Designed by Shanghai architect Xing Tonghe, the futuristic building with a circular roof with four decorative holders is said to resemble an ancient bronze seen from a distance. Six stone lions and two stone *bixie*, mythical Chinese beasts, guard the entrance to the museum and the granite walls of the building are decorated with designs found in ancient bronzeware.

With an exhibition space more than three times greater than the former building, the 29.5 metre (97 feet) structure has seven levels, two being underground. From the ground floor to the fourth floor are 14 showrooms for sculptures, paintings, calligraphy, coins, ceramics, ancient bronzes, jadeware and national minority handicrafts. Research facilities will be afforded on the top floor. Part of the underground section houses a multi-purpose hall complete with the most up-to-date audio and visual facilities installed.

Shanghai Natural History Museum

Located at 260 Yanan Dong Lu, just a few blocks southwest of the Peace Hotel, this museum was built in 1956 and boasts an extensive collection of ancient and modern exhibits. There are always specific exhibitions going on, some of which are interesting in a more general way, and there are also small permanent collections on view. Among the exhibits is the fossil of a 140-million-year-old dinosaur from Sichuan Province. The museum is open 8.30 am–10.30 am and 1.30 pm–4 pm.

Shanghai Exhibition Centre

This vast hall in Yanan Zhong Lu, built in 1955 very much in the style of the Beijing Exhibition Centre, was first known as the Palace of Sino-Soviet Friendship. With its high, gilded steel spire tapering to a red star, and its cavernous interior, it is distinctly reminiscent of Soviet baroque (or 'wedding-cake') in its style.

Several large sections of the building are given over to domestic and international trade shows and industrial exhibits from time to time. These are generally not open to the public and are not of much interest to the average tourist: themes run from 'East China Textiles' to 'Printing Technology', although at times fashion, houseware, gift shows and interesting displays of light industrial products are held.

Two sections of the U-shaped centre house tourist shops selling an impressive

THE SOONG FAMILY

The Soongs were a parvenu Shanghai family. The father, Charlie Soong, had been brought up and educated in the United States, and had returned to Shanghai as a Southern Methodist. He had intended to work for a missionary, but instead had prospered through printing bibles. He fathered six children, the most famous of whom were the three daughters—Ai-ling, Ching-ling and May-ling—and their brother T V.

The children grew up in a YMCA atmosphere; the three girls attended the Methodist Mctyeire School on Yuyuan Lu, and were then sent to study at the Weslyan College for Women in the United States. T V (who, as was the fashion in Shanghai, was always called by his Anglicized initials rather than by his Chinese name), went to Harvard and Columbia.

A regular visitor to the Soong home was Sun Yat-sen, to whose revolutionary ideals Charlie Soong was sympathetic. The ties which bound the two men were made even more intimate when the future father of the Chinese republic married the revolutionary-minded Ching-ling, in spite of

(left) Song Ching-ling and Dr Sun Yat-sen shortly after their marriage, 1915
(below) Soong May-ling

his being the same age as her father and already married to another woman.

Ai-ling had married Dr H H Kung, the scion of a substantial banking family and a descendant of Confucius. It was a successful alliance, for Ai-ling had a good nose for money and Dr Kung was to become the Minister of Finance in the Guomindang (Kuomintang) government.

Whenever China purchased a military aircraft, it was said, Madame Kung invariably received a considerable commission from the sale.

Upward mobility was in the family, and if Ai-ling married into the highest circles of society, her sister May-ling became China's First Lady. To win May-ling, Chiang Kai-shek, who was 13 years older and who was to become China's supreme leader, not only disposed of an earlier wife and the mother of his son (Chiang Ching-kuo, the late leader of Taiwan), but also agreed to be converted to Methodism.

In her instinct for power, Soong May-ling stands in the line of Empress Wu and Madame Mao; in her limitless greed, she is perhaps rivalled only by Imelda Marcos. Like her sister Ai-ling and her brother T V (who also became Minister of Finance under Chiang Kai-shek), Soong May-ling amassed a fabulous personal fortune by manipulating government bonds, speculating in silver and currency, and siphoning off American aid. By the time the Communists came, they had already stashed away millions of dollars in American banks.

Only Ching-ling remained in China after the Communist triumph. Aptly, the Chinese say of the Soong sisters that 'Ai-ling loved money, May-ling loved power, and Ching-ling loved China.'

Sketchers in China depicting the infamous opium trade, Illustrated London News, *1883*

Packing.

range of clothing, arts and crafts, rugs, jewellery and gift items. The two sections are not connected, however, and it is necessary to cross the parking lot to gain entrance to both of them. Taking the first entrance on the left and climbing the stairs leads you to one of the most impressive displays of master craftsmen's work, including handicrafts and superb examples of traditional Chinese furniture. Prices are well beyond the reach of the average mortal, but the display is well worth looking at.

SHANGHAI ART MUSEUM

Located at 456 Nanjing Xi Lu, next to the Shanghai Acrobatics Theatre, the museum hosts an interesting selection of temporary exhibitions. Though concentrating on modern Chinese art, with occasional photographic displays, recent exhibitions have included paintings by aboriginal artists and a large display of oil paintings by Renaissance masters. The museum is open from 9.30 am–4 pm daily. Admission is as little as 2 *yuan*. The Art Museum is to be rehoused in the old Race Club building facing People's Park, which was previously occupied by the Shanghai Library.

SHANGHAI HISTORY MUSEUM

Located at 1286 Hongqiao Lu, this new museum houses a fascinating collection of objects depicting the development of Shanghai under foreign domination. There are around 1000 exhibits from the 1860 to 1949 period, including many old maps and photographs of the International Settlement and the French Concession, many objets d'art and remnants of the fallen glories of imperialism, such as a stone lion which used to stand outside the Hongkong and Shanghai Bank building. The museum is open daily from 9 am–4 pm.

Shanghai also has some smaller galleries and exhibitions. There are occasional exhibitions at the **Shanghai University Fine Arts Institute**, 30 Kaixuan Lu. For those interested in ceramics there is the **Hanguang Pottery Art Gallery**, 900 Wanping Nan Lu. There are a number of private exhibitions often housed in people's homes which can be visited by appointment. Collections include fans, butterflies, ancient jars and cases, theatrical costumes and miniature musical instruments. Contact the Shanghai Municipal Administration, or CITS, for advice.

Other Places Of Interest

THE PORT OF SHANGHAI

Shanghai is China's pre-eminent industrial centre, but it is also its chief trading port, with wharves stretching 56 kilometres (35 miles) along the wide, muddy Huangpu

River. The great central waterway of China, the Yangzi (Yangtse) River, is little more than ten kilometres (six miles) north of the city, and not only links Shanghai with important cities of China's interior—Nanjing (Nanking), Wuhan, and Chongqing (Chungking)—but also connects Shanghai to the Yellow Sea.

It has been estimated that Shanghai handles a third of China's seagoing freight (in excess of 100 million tons a year), and extensive redevelopment plans will greatly increase the port's capacity. There are four container terminals in the port, one of them installed with computer systems. A modern seaway is being constructed to allow ships of about 50,000 tons to enter the harbour.

■ **River Excursion:** It is difficult for foreign tourists to see much of the dock area, but the three-and-a-half hour river trip down to the mouth of the Yangzi, on cruise boats which leave from Shiliupu Pier, provides an opportunity for looking at Shanghai's port facilities. Tickets are on sale on the second floor of the Boat Ticket Office at the corner of Jinling Lu and the Bund. The price of the first-class ticket includes snacks and tea. There are two excursions a day, one in the morning (departing at 9.00 am) and one in the afternoon (at 2.00 pm). To these an evening cruise is added in the summer months (7.00 pm).

This is what passengers sailing down the Huangpu River from the Bund will see: Huangpu Park, Suzhou Creek with the Waibaidu Bridge arching over it, Shanghai Mansions, the International Passenger Terminal, the Yangpu bridge, the Shanghai Shipyard, the Yangshupu Power Plant, Fuxing Islet (Shanghai's oldest industrial estate and China's first container terminal), the site of the Wusong Fort, and finally, beyond the Wusong (the mouth of the confluence of the Huangpu and the Yangzi), the mingling of the heavily silted water of the river with the clearer water of the sea. The high point of the trip for many passengers is the return journey, when the boat sails into the Shanghai harbour and the line of buildings on the Bund comes into view. The trip impresses upon one the importance of river and sea trade to Shanghai's growth— from being a mere fishing village to being the gateway of China.

THE PUDONG NEW AREA

Pudong, the city of the future, lies on the other side of the Huangpu River to the old International Settlement. The cityscape is dominated by the 468 metre (1550 feet) high Shanghai 'Oriental Pearl' television and communication tower. The love-it-or-hate-it pinnacle has viewing areas for spectacular panorama's of the harbour and the old city areas. Work is also underway on the construction of the International Country Club and Pearl Amusement Park in the Huaxia Tourism Development Zone.

The two bridges which link Pudong with the downtown area have sidewalks and elevators for the use of sightseers—again with great views. The Nanpu bridge, with a central span of 423 metres (1400 feet), was opened in 1991 and the Yangpu bridge,

The Oriental Pearl TV Tower, Pudong New Area

with a central span of 602 metres (1950 feet), was opened in 1993. Taking a taxi or bus across one of the bridges is a less strenuous option. A fun way to cross to Pudong is on the crowded ferry from the dock along the Bund at Yanan Dong Lu (for more information on Pudong see page 114).

Municipal Children's Palace (Shi Shaonian Gong)

In a scheme to allow children a chance to develop interests outside their school work— whether it be painting, music, computers, model-aeroplanes, electronics, gymnastics, table-tennis or ballet—children's 'palaces' have been developed in Chinese cities. Each of Shanghai's 12 urban districts runs a palace where children go for several hours a week after school, and there is one run by the municipality. The palaces are staffed by volunteer school teachers, as well as some full-time instructors.

A visit to one of the palaces is a particularly enjoyable part of any tour itinerary in Shanghai. Visitors usually watch some of the children's classes and are then given a display of some sort by the children. The palaces vary enormously in quality and facilities, and in the kind of child that attends. Obviously the local palaces, run by the districts, will not be nearly as well-equipped as the one run by the municipality. The latter, an organ of the China Welfare Institute founded by the late Soong Ching-ling, occupies the grand mansion where the influential and wealthy Kadoorie family of Hong Kong used to live. Many of the children who attend have been hand-picked for their outstanding abilities, and it is here that you will come across those widely publicized little child prodigies. This palace is at 64 Yanan Xi Lu, directly across from the Hotel Equatorial. Visits can be arranged directly (tel. 258-1850) or through CITS. Visits should be made in the late afternoon or on Sundays.

Markets

An interesting fish and flower market is held in an alley between Jiangyin Lu and Huangpi Bei Lu and is easily reached from Renmin Square. Peddlers sit behind buckets and basins containing goldfish and other kinds of pet fish, as well as fish feed. Other stands offer potted plants, flower pots and fertilizers. On average, 300 stalls do 1,500 *yuan*'s worth of business a day. As the prices are not fixed, it is possible to bargain, this being one of the 'free markets' operating outside the state economy. The Huating Market is also run by private traders. There are stalls selling clothes, fish, meat, fruit and vegetables and several dumpling stalls, situated in a section of Hua Ting Lu, off Huaihai Zhong Lu. For the antiques markets, refer to page 48.

Great World (Dashijie)

The spire of the Great World Entertainment Centre, festooned with advertisements for detergents and electrical appliances, is a distinctive landmark south of Renmin

Square. The building stands at the busy junction of Xizang Zhong Lu and Yanan Lu, which is straddled by an overhead walkway. Now the Youth Palace, although the name *Dashijie* is still emblazoned above its entrance, the Great World once represented all the decadence and sordidness of old Shanghai. Here, in the 1930s, gambling dens, massage parlours, brothels, dance halls and restaurants drew every variety of pleasure-seeker and hedonist. Today it houses video arcades, outdoor theatres, discos, restaurants and cafés.

Shanghai Zoo (Shanghai Dongwuyuan)
This is located in the western suburbs of the city on Hongqiao Lu. Before 1949, it was the city's main golf course but was converted in 1954 into a zoo with an area of 70 hectares (173 acres). The zoo houses some 350 species of animals and birds, both native to China and foreign. A great draw for visitors is of course the Giant Panda.

Parks

Fuxing Park
This attractive park is situated in the south-central section of the city; take a left into Chongqing Lu from Huaihai Zhong Lu and you will find the park further down on the left. The park was built in 1909 and has some notable features which make it outstanding among Shanghai's major parks. There are massive trees which provide good shade during the hot summer months. There is also a small zoo. In the early morning the park is full of activity with people of all ages jogging and practising *taijiquan*. During the afternoons elderly people play cards and Chinese chess while women look after small children. Parks are always a good place to meet locals, and here you may encounter Shanghainese, both young and old, keen to practise their English. For those staying at the Jinjiang Hotel the park is just a short walk away.

Guilin Park
Located in the southwestern suburbs, the park was built in 1933 in the grounds of Huang Jinrong's house. Huang Jinrong was a confederate of the gangster Du Yue-sheng (see page 72). The park is built in the Suzhou style and is a very pleasant place to spend part of your morning or afternoon.

Hongkou Park
Laid out in 1905, this park was once part of the Japanese section of the city. Today it houses the Lu Xun Memorial (see page 69). There are rowing boats for hire here but it is often difficult to get one since demand greatly exceeds the supply. Occasionally

lantern exhibitions are held in the park and in the autumn large crowds turn out to view the spectacular chrysanthemum show.

Huangpu Park

This occupies a corner of the foreshore to the southeast of Waibaidu Bridge. It was first laid out, back in the days of the foreign concessions, by the British, who called it the Public Gardens and restricted its use to Europeans only. Apart from Chinese nannies, the natives were supposedly barred from the park by an infamous sign 'No dogs and Chinese allowed'. In fact, no such sign existed, although two of the garden's regulations, posted on a board at the entrance, did indeed discriminate against dogs and Chinese. There are paths through the gardens and plenty of benches where you can spend a relaxing afternoon.

Renmin Park And Renmin Square

The concentration of shops in Nanjing Lu is relieved by the greenery of Renmin (People's) Park. Laid out on what used to be the British-run racecourse, the park is a pleasant 12-hectare (30-acre) oasis of trees, pools and decorative rocks. The old Race Club building, with its distinctive clock tower and extensive grandstand which until recently housed the city library, is to be the new venue for the Shanghai Art Museum. A new library will be opened in 1996 at the intersection of Huaihai Zhong Lu and Gao'an Lu.

On the south side of the park is the enormous Renmin Square. Laid out in 1951, the square has undergone a dramatic transformation over the last few years. The renovated square, which still incorporates a large area of green space, was officially re-opened in September 1994. The square now houses the magnificent new Shanghai Museum and the Shanghai Municipal Hall. The latter, a 20 storey building, has two exhibition rooms on Shanghai's historical, cultural and economic developments. An underground shopping area, car park and metro station can also be found in the square.

Shanghai Botanical Gardens

Located in the southwest of the city at 1100 Longwu Lu, the garden is considered to be one of the best in China. Covering an area of 70 hectares (25 acres) the garden has five sections, including *bonsais*, miniature potted landscapes and a corridor of potted stone mountain landscapes as well as magnificent orchid displays in season.

Xijiao (Western Suburbs) Park

The park lies in the far west of the city, quite near Hongqiao Airport and not far from the Shanghai Zoo. It is a delightful park where few foreigners ever venture. There are

The Shanghai Persona

It has long been a cliché that the cleverest people in China come from Shanghai, but when the British Consul-General asked the mayor of Shanghai if this generalization was true, the answer he got was, 'No, the cleverest people come *to* Shanghai'.

The mayor has a point: Shanghai is a melting pot. Even the most Shanghainese of Shanghai families have come not all that long ago from somewhere else. The Shanghainese has something of many regions in China. Yet, for all that he/she is of 'motley' stock, the Shanghainese has a distinct identity.

But the Shanghainese have not always had the same image. In the second half of the 19th century, they compared unfavourably with the Cantonese, whose city was the first port in China to be opened to foreign trade, and who were thus the first people to gain any familiarity with Western ways. This was how three Europeans wrote of the people of Shanghai when they arrived at the port in the mid-1800s: 'The natives of this part of China appear as nearly devoid of intellect as is compatible with the existence of human conformation. In this respect, as in their lighter complexion and manner of dressing (especially in the particular of wearing shoes and stockings, and long gowns instead of jackets), the Shanghai Chinese differ from the brisk and handy natives of the South.'

The love of dress has persisted, but the rest of the image has changed with time. As the foreigner and native found a common interest in the pursuit of profit in the foreign concessions, it began to be felt that the Shanghainese were almost too clever. Several lasting traits, many of them exemplified by the compradore, were initiated during this period. A bent for money-making and an admiration of things Western became part of the Shanghai persona.

A unique but short-lived creation of Shanghai was true biculturalism, something no other Chinese community, not even Hong Kong, has succeeded in producing. Before the Communist revolution locked China into her own culture, there grew up in Shanghai a class of people who could truly take on the manners and thinking of another culture without the debasement of their own.

Most things in China reach their apogee in Shanghai—capitalism in the pre-revolution period, Gang-of-Fourism during the Cultural Revolution. It is no wonder the Shanghainese think themselves special—they have dictated fashion to China for decades and continue to do so. How all this will affect business and social relations with the new foreign adventurer and entrepreneur—only time will tell.

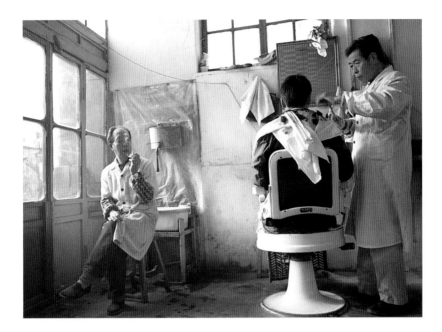

*At the hairdressers—a contrast of generations as older men repeat the habits of a life-time
while prospective brides sit through the essential modern coiffure treatment*

SHANGHAI ARCHITECTURE

*Tess Johnston and
Peter Hibbard*

If ever a city's architecture should be called *fin de siècle*, it is Shanghai's. Parts of metropolitan Shanghai resemble a city suspended in 1937, when the Japanese occupied the whole city except for the French Concession and the International Settlement. With the Japanese takeover of these foreign enclaves in December 1941, all Western life—and all building projects—stopped. Foreigners returning to Shanghai after 1945 found themselves to be strangers in a city that was once theirs, with many of their architectural triumphs turned to white elephants.

Since then much of the downtown area has remained unchanged, especially the Bund, though major pockets of modern redevelopment have resulted in the destruction of many pre-war buildings. Somewhat like a dentist pulling teeth, the developers' crane and bulldozer are increasingly crawling over the Shanghai landscape.

Modern Shanghai could be summed up by a British visitor who said that it resembled a cross between Warsaw 1933, Calcutta and Hong Kong. In the area stretching from the world-famous Bund waterfront westward, into the former French and International settlements, you had a city of primarily Western architecture, increasingly peppered with modern pinnacles, with a Chinese population dropped into it—at about 300% of saturation point!

It is true that there are areas of this city that have Chinese architecture. The area north of the Bund and the egg-shaped 'native city', as it used to be called, abound in low wooden houses with tiled roofs; its alleys are barely the width of your outstretched arms. This 'native city' or 'old town' is an area of several square miles surrounded by a ring-road laid over what used to be the city walls and moat. In the old days you needed a guide just to enter its perilous streets. Now the streets around its old Temple of the Town God (Chenghuang Miao) hum with foreign tourists as well as Chinese shoppers, and the Bridge of Nine Turnings leading to Huxinting, the teahouse of willow-pattern fame, is surrounded by camera buffs of all nationalities.

Still, these are not the places that people generally think of when they conjure up a vision of Shanghai as the Paris of the East. Rather, they dwell on the cosmopolitan aspect of Shanghai in its heyday. And this image of a cosmopolitan city, dominated as it was by Western architecture, is even more remarkable when you consider that at no time did Westerners constitute more than 10% of its vast population. But it was this minority of Westerners who held the power, through the Municipal Council, and who could construct buildings primarily to their own taste—when they were not making a quick profit by building high-density housing for the Chinese population. (It is interesting to note that the basis of many of the fortunes amassed by the Westerners was derived from real estate speculation.)

All the major *hongs* (Western companies) had their offices on or near the Bund, and each tried to outdo the other in erecting an imposing edifice, designed to resemble the buildings in their countries of origin. Dominating the Bund was the Hongkong and Shanghai Bank building, housing on the ground floor its own bank, the largest in the Far East. It was completed in 1923 and was famous not only for its imposing architecture but also for the two brass lions outside the main entrance. Their noses were kept glistening by being stroked repeatedly by Chinese passers-by, who hoped thereby to improve their luck. These lions disappeared during the Cultural Revolution— but are rumoured to exist still in some dusty warehouse. Only time will tell...

Sharing the glory as the best of the Bund is the Customs House, built next door in 1927. Its tower clock 'Big Ching' has spawned this story: after it was erected, the number of fires in the city declined. The Chinese thus believed that its chiming confused the God of Fire. When he heard its bells every quarter hour, he thought it was a fire bell and decided that Shanghai had enough fires already so he did not have to send more.

During the Cultural Revolution the bell was replaced by a loudspeaker which played *The East is Red*. Now, alas, the clock's chime is so weak that it is drowned by the traffic noise of the Bund.

Also sharing places of honour on the Bund were both haunts of Western residents and visitors: the Cathay and Palace hotels, and the Shanghai Club, reputedly containing the longest bar in the world. Part of the latter is now a ubiquitous Kentucky Fried Chicken outlet, while the two former British hotels are the north and south wings of the Peace Hotel.

The glory of the old hotels is, however, undimmed, and several have been renovated to something resembling their old splendour.

The Peace still leads the way, having based its renovation on the original plans, but the Park on Nanjing Lu and the Cathay Mansions and old Grosvenor House (now the Jinjiang Hotel) evoke only a slightly dimmer version of the days of their glorious past. Opposite, the famous old Cercle Sportif Français has been incorporated into the lobby of the Garden Hotel and beautifully restored. And no matter what their current state, these magnificent old hotels and clubs could never be accused by anyone of being Plastic City.

Leading off the Bund to the west are four major streets, originally called Horse Roads Nos 1, 2, 3 and 4. No 1, or 'Da Ma Lu' is Nanjing Lu, the best and most famous shopping street in all of China. (It is said that visitors from the provinces and even from Beijing always come to Shanghai with empty suitcases—and pooled cash resourses.)

All the major department store chains had their most prestigious shops here—Sun Sun, Wing On, Sun and Sincere. These stores have been recently changed almost beyond recognition, though apart from the new

Colonial architecture in Shanghai

glass face of the former Wing On Store (now the Huilian Department
Store), the upper façades offer reminders of the hazy past. A visitor step-
ping out of a time warp would have little trouble locating Whiteway and
Laidlaw or the Sun (now the No 1 Department store) at the corner of
Tibet (Xizang) and Nanjing roads, where reportedly a million shoppers
now pass each day.

As you proceed westward the stores are interspersed with large apartment blocks, many in the Art Deco style of the Twenties and Thirties.
(The only other city that contains as many is Miami Beach, Florida.)
These apartment buildings all had elegant (or sometimes descriptive)
names: The Uptown, The West Gardens, Holly Heath, Tiny Mansions. A
newly completed listing contains nearly 300 names, starting with Aida
(on Rue Cardinal Mercier, now Maoming Lu) and ending with Ziccawei,
where the Jesuits once reigned with their schools, orphanages and office
buildings in Italianate ecclesiastical style.

The stores and apartment houses gradually give way to the mansions
of the former *taipans*, the top echelon of Shanghai's business hierarchy.
These magnificent estates usually featured large south-facing gardens
(now overbuilt with housing for the city's work-force) and ranged in style
from Gothic fantasy (the Moller House on Yanan Lu) to a mock Tudor
country estate (the Sassoon villa on Hongqiao Lu). Between these extremes were numerous mansions in the French, Spanish and English
styles, homes of expatriate barons and dukes, big gangster bosses and
Kuomintang high brass. Today they are occupied by the offices (or officials) of the current Chinese power structure.

The greatest architectural treats can be seen primarily by looking
upward. The lower level of Shanghai's architectural treasures is all too
often obscured by recent modifications (the ubiquitous smoked glass, for
example), or by the tenants' laundry, drying fish or other impedimenta
that inevitably hang from Chinese window poles. But above all the urban
squalor that any city produces you find the bones of the beauty that once
was Shanghai's: cream-coloured tiles, della Robbia wreaths of plaster,
stucco and half-timbered overhangs, Corinthian columns supporting
elaborate friezes. Covered with industrial grime, to be sure, and suffering
from decades of benign neglect, these architectural relics nevertheless
shine like nuggets of gold through the dross of China's biggest, busiest
and most fascinating city.

a number of small lakes and pavilions where it is pleasant just to sit and escape from the din and pollution of the city. There is also a roller-skating rink for those who feel they need the exercise or just fancy a little fun.

ZHONGSHAN PARK

Lying to the west of the city and built in 1914, this park was known to Shanghai's Chinese residents as Caofeng Park and to its foreign residents as Jessfield Park. The park contains a peony garden, and also a rose garden with more than 200 species of this flower. Before 1949, a corner of the park formed the campus of St John's University, Shanghai's first university. Today, the buildings house the Huadong Institute of Politics and Law.

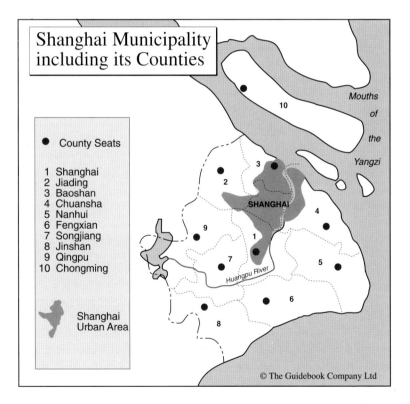

Shanghai Municipality
including its Counties

Mouths
of
the
Yangzi

● County Seats

1 Shanghai
2 Jiading
3 Baoshan
4 Chuansha
5 Nanhui
6 Fengxian
7 Songjiang
8 Jinshan
9 Qingpu
10 Chongming

SHANGHAI

Huangpu River

Shanghai
Urban Area

© The Guidebook Company Ltd

Sights Outside Shanghai

Those staying a while in Shanghai, or those wishing to escape the rush of city life, might find a visit to one of the outlying counties a worthwhile experience. The journey offers a chance to look at the surrounding countryside and towns, and there are also some interesting temples and pagodas to see. Transport by public bus takes 1–3 hours depending on the traffic and the distance you are going.

Shanghai as a municipality consists of not just the urban core, but a large part of the countryside around it. It is really a city-region, a series of concentric zones expanding out from the urban centre to the suburbs and the surrounding country, with rural counties like Jiading and Qingpu forming the outer ring. So even when you travel out to the country and think you have left Shanghai behind, you haven't. The idea behind creating city-regions was to ensure the inner city a reliable supply of food and water, and enough space for the city's industrial and residential expansion.

One reason for Shanghai's great economic success over the past 30 years has in fact been the considerable support given by its rural counties. Under the new economic measures, which privatized farming and strengthened market forces, these have become some of the most prosperous places in the country. The tourist driving out into the country will not miss the new private houses and factories going up everywhere, or the obvious productivity of the land.

JIADING COUNTY

Lying about 19 kilometres (12 miles) to the northwest of Shanghai proper, Jiading is one of the municipality's rising counties. To get to Jiading by public transport, take the bus from the Northern Bus Station, situated on Gonghexin Lu at the corner of Zhongshan Bei Lu.

The **Confucian Temple** on Nanda Jie is well worth visiting. The Confucian temple in China used to serve a dual function: as a place for performing sacrifices to the sage and as a hall where county and prefectural examinations were held. This one was begun in 1218 during the Southern Song Dynasty (1127–1279) and then restructured between 1241 and 1252. Over the centuries it has been extended and reconstructed. In 1958, it was restored and now the wings of the main hall, which contain memorial tablets, make up the County Museum.

Three memorial arches stand before the temple. The stone balustrades between the arches are decorated with 72 stone lions symbolizing the 72 worthy disciples of Confucius. The main gate bears a Yuan Dynasty stone sculpture of fish and dragon—an allusion to the Chinese expression 'a carp leaping over the Dragon Gate' for career advancement, and an auspicious omen for all of the examination candidates passing through the gate.

Over the pond, the visitor arrives at Dazhen Gate. This is flanked by seven stone turtles each bearing a stone tablet on its back inscribed with a history of the temple.

Another of Jiading's historical relics is the **Fahua Pagoda**. This Buddhist pagoda was built during the Southern Song Dynasty. The pagoda fell into serious disrepair during the Qing Dynasty (1644–1911) and it was not until 1919 that the structure was rebuilt again using concrete and iron. The pagoda is not on the usual tour itineraries but if you are in the area it is worth a look.

■ **Nanxiang:** A town in Jiading County, Nanxiang is 17 kilometres (ten-and-a-half miles) to the northwest of downtown Shanghai. Nanxiang is linked in most Shanghainese minds with those small steamed dumplings that you can buy in the Old Town (see page 56). If you find yourself in the vicinity, take a walk in the **Guyi Garden**, which was first laid out in the Ming Dynasty (1368–1644), and later rebuilt in the Qianlong period (1736–1796). It has been renovated and extended since 1949, and now covers six-and-a-half hectares (16 acres). The garden still retains features of the traditional Chinese garden in its pavilions, lakes, corridors, winding paths and bridges, and it has its own version of the famous marble boat in Beijing's Summer Palace. Known as the 'United Boat', this is a small pavilion in the shape of a boat, built on a stone base in one of the garden's lakes.

■ **Zhenru:** The **Zhenru Temple**, built in 1320, is to be found on Nanda Jie in Zhenru, another of Jiading County's small towns. Most of the present temple buildings date from the Yuan Dynasty (1279–1368) but there have been a few additions. When the temple was restored in 1963 it was discovered that many of the original craftsmen working on the temple had written their names and their positions on the wooden parts of the structure. The writing is now an important source material for those studying calligraphy. The building as a whole is a fine example of 14th-century architecture and provides much information on old construction techniques.

JINSHAN COUNTY

Jinshan, one of Shanghai Municipality's rural counties, lies to the southwest of the city two hours by car. It is in Songwen, a town in the county, that the **Huayan Pagoda** is to be found. In the Yuan Dynasty (1279–1368) the pagoda began life as a Buddhist monastery. The monks there wrote the Huayan classics in 81 volumes and it was with the proceeds from the sales that the pagoda was built. The pagoda took four years to build and was completed in the early Ming Dynasty in 1380. It is a brick and wooden structure which, if you are travelling down the Huangpu River, you can see towering over the south bank. The pagoda is worth looking at since it remains one of the best examples of the kind of construction work done during the Ming Dynasty and it is almost completely preserved. Take the bus for Jinshan from the Western Bus Station at 240 Caoxi Bei Lu.

Qingpu County farmer

■ ZHUJING

The Jinshan Academy of Farmers' Painting is to be found in the southwestern county town of Zhujing. A large collection of gouache paintings in the gallery are available for sale at around 300 *yuan* each. The academy, situated at 318 Jiankang Lu, is open from 8 am–5 pm.

QINGPU COUNTY

Qingpu County is some 22.5 kilometres (14 miles) to the west of Shanghai. During the Tang (618–907) and Song (960–1127) Dynasties, the county seat was a flourishing market and port where merchants gathered to carry on local and foreign trade. It was so busy that the town became known as Little Hangzhou (a famous resort to Shanghai's south and the capital of Zhejiang Province), and in the surrounding area shrines and temples proliferated. Later, the area around Qingpu fell into disuse as a market and business centre, and the temples and shrines gradually disappeared, leaving just one pagoda to bear witness to the area's rich history. Today, Qingpu is Shanghai's main supplier of freshwater fish. To get to Qingpu take the bus from the Western Bus Station at 240 Caoxi Bei Lu.

■ DAYING LAKE

When they are in Qingpu, Shanghainese sightseers go to the **Qushui Yuan** (the Garden of Meandering Stream), which is to be found on the shore of Daying Lake, in the northeast corner of the county seat. Originally called the Ling Garden, the Qushui was completed in 1745 during the reign of the famous emperor, Qianlong. In the garden there are several scenic spots, and in the northern part a hill from which not only the garden but the surrounding hills can be viewed. In 1927 the garden was redeveloped and changed its name to Zhongshan Garden, but basically the style and features remain those of the old garden.

■ DIANSHAN LAKE

Some 50 kilometres (31 miles) from Shanghai, this huge lake in the upper reaches of the Huangpu River is a source of the city's drinking water. With an area 12 times larger than the famous West Lake of Hangzhou, it teems with carp, mandarin fish, freshwater shrimps and crabs. A holiday resort, covering an area of just under 90 hectares (222 acres), has been developed near **Yangshe Village**, on the southeastern stretch of the lake. A park named after the famous garden of the classic Chinese novel, *The Dream of the Red Chamber*, the **Prospect Garden** (Daguanyuan), has been laid out. The imitation pavilions and cottages are in rather bad taste, but are popular with sightseers. Streets and houses modelled on those of ancient Chinese towns are planned, as are numerous amusement parks and sanatoria. A number of restaurants offer dishes cooked with the lake's live produce.

■ QINGLONG

Near the ancient town of Qinglong in Qingpu County, just over half a mile from the old Qingpu town, stands the **Qinglong Pagoda** (known also as the Jinyu Monastery Pagoda). In 743 Baode Temple was built and the Qinglong Pagoda was added in 821. At the same time the temple was renamed 'Longdu'. The last major restructuring of the pagoda was during the Northern Song in 1041–48 when the temple changed its name again to Jingyu Monastery. The original structure was of brick and wood but today it is all brick and in the style of the Song Dynasty.

SONGJIANG COUNTY

Songjiang is a county 19 kilometres (12 miles) southeast of Shanghai, on the railway line to Hangzhou. The county town was founded under the Sui Dynasty (581–618) and was known at that time for a delicate fish known as a Song perch or Song *lu*. Visitors who have the time might enjoy making a trip out there and taking a look at the **Square Pagoda** (Fang Ta) which stands in the southeast of the town. Belonging once to the Xingshengjiao Temple, the nine-storey pagoda was built in the Song Dynasty (960–1279). The pagoda is architecturally interesting because although it was restored in 1975, much of the original 11th-century brick and wood structure remains. Of the 1778 wooden brackets supporting the eaves, 60 per cent date back to the Song Dynasty.

Beside the pagoda stands a large **Screen Wall**, another of Songjiang's historical relics. Erected in 1370 during the reign of the Ming Emperor Hongwu, it is decorated with a massive brick bas-relief, six metres (20 feet) long and 4.5 metres (15 feet) across. It depicts an imposing legendary beast, the 'monster of avarice', which apparently tried to eat everything on earth, and finally drowned by rushing into the sea to swallow it up. The monster is surrounded by intricate patterns of flowers, trees, rocks, and animals. The beast is called Tan, a homonym of the Chinese word for 'greedy'. Also depicted are various scenes symbolizing human ambitions—a carp leaping over the Dragon Gate is a Chinese metaphor for promotion to high office, a lotus blossom growing beside a vase with three lances suggests advancing by three grades of office, a monkey jumping to snatch a gold seal hanging from a tree symbolizes the desire to become a prince. The moral to be drawn from the bas-relief is that it doesn't pay to be too over-ambitious.

■ SHESHAN (SHE HILL)

A small hill, 100 metres (328 feet) above sea level, to the west of the city, Sheshan is 17 kilometres (10.5 miles) north of Songjiang Town. Local lore has it that a hermit by the name of She once lived in the hill. Sheshan is renowned for its bamboo groves, but its greatest interest for the foreign tourist lies in the **basilica** that crowns the hill—the largest Roman Catholic cathedral in East Asia.

THE PEASANT PAINTERS OF JINSHAN

It all started when a demobbed soldier returned to his native home in Jin-shan County. His attention was caught by the way the village women there decorated their kerchiefs, aprons, clothes, pillow cases, hats, shoes and *dudou* ('belly-cloths'). There was something about their sense of colour, and the way they worked the traditional motifs into their craft, which suggested to the soldier that they might, with a little bit of instruction, become good painters. It was only a matter of substituting the needles, cloths, threads and scissors with painting brushes, paints and canvas.

Though some of the women can barely write their own names, they turn out the most wonderful paintings, full of colour, life, and detail. Untutored as painters, the women have nevertheless been working with their fingers—be it spinning, weaving, cutting paper into pictures, doing needlework, making clay toys or decorating their homes—most of their lives. And it proves easy to transfer these skills from one medium into another. The decorative patterns were already there, in the traditional design of local cloth, in the *nianhua* (the New Year pictures) that the Chinese have always liked to hang up, in the lanterns and kites that they have been making for generations. Naive and exuberantly coloured, the pictures demonstrate the country women's love of the decorative, and portray the rustic, everyday concerns of their lives and society.

Because the painters understand so prolifically the roles they embody—as grandmothers and mothers—the scenes depicted are usually domestic ones: weddings, the kitchen, celebrating a newborn baby's first month, ducks and hens, fish and shrimps, crabs and turtles, harvest and markets. Typically a picture shows a village jetty from which a bride is leaving with her dowry. Trumpeters and musicians play. A crowd watches in curiosity. Poignantly, in the backyard, the mother who is about to be parted from her daughter sheds tears.

Another picture shows a woman entering her kitchen with an exaggerat-edly large fish in one hand and a cleaver in another. More than half the picture is taken up by the stove, which is decorated with scenes from famil-iar operas: Liu Hai Teasing the Golden Toad, The Butterfly Lovers and Zhang Fei Challenges Ma Chao.

The attention to detail (a feminine trait?) is charming. In a painting of a fish market, the artist has not neglected to include an abacus, and a couple of steelyards for weighing the fish. Other pictures are elaborations of symmetrical patterns combining naturalistic and abstract fragments.

When the demobilized soldier introduced the paint brush to the country folk of Jinshan, it was the older women, the ones with a lifetime of embroidery and lace-making behind them, who first took it up. But later they were joined by younger women, and now people of all ages paint in Jinshan. Their reputation has grown, so that now their pictures have been exhibited both at home and abroad.

The One-month-old Baby, *a painting depicting one of the happiest days in the life of a grandmother, who is also the painter. Preparations are underway for the celebration— a feast of fish, chicken, and a nourishing soup for the mother.*

In 1844, French Roman Catholic missionaries came here and bought some land on the southern slopes of the hill. The succeeding years saw the building of a chapel and the growth of a Catholic community here, and in 1871 a cathedral was erected at the top of the hill. The building which stands today is a later construction, begun in 1925 and completed ten years later. A niche in the roof contained a statue of the Madonna and Child, but this was destroyed in the Cultural Revolution and is now replaced with a large cross. A seminary was built in 1983 and the cathedral has once more become a place of worship. The walls inside the basilica are hung with pictures of the Fourteen Stations of the Cross. An observatory, built by the Jesuits, stands near the church. On the hill leading to it is a small chapel, the Zhongshan Chapel. Many of the devotees who worship at the church believe that the Virgin Mary appeared on Sheshan in 1980.

Tea Garden and pavilion in Shanghai, Illustrated London News, *1863*

Excursions From Shanghai

'Above there is heaven; on earth there are Suzhou and Hangzhou.' So goes the old Chinese saying. No one today could call either of these cities a paradise on earth, but they are refreshing escapes from Shanghai's urban pressures.

■ HANGZHOU

Hangzhou's fabled West Lake is probably China's best-known beauty spot. The air is clean, the landscape green and tranquil, and the avenues of willows and arched stone bridges conform to everyone's idea of what Chinese scenery should look like.

Two of Hangzhou's hotels offer services of international standard: the 388-room **Shangri-La Hotel** (78 Beishan Lu. Tel. 777951), and the 549-room **Dragon Hotel** (Shuguang Lu. Tel. 554488), which is managed by New World Hotels International.

The staff of the hotels will, if advised, meet you at the airport (it is a 30-minute flight from Shanghai) or the railway station (three to four hours, depending on which train you take). The hotels will also help with transport back to Shanghai. (You can't book and pay for return transportation in China.)

■ SUZHOU

Suzhou is much nearer to Shanghai (two hours by car; 90 minutes by train) and thus makes an agreeable day's outing should you want to take a closer look at the Chinese art of creating gardens.

As China's most famous garden city, Suzhou has managed to retain its heritage with 100 gardens of various sizes. Like paintings and ceramics, it is an art form at which the Chinese excel and Suzhou's evocatively named Garden of the Master of Nets, Pavilion of the Waves, Humble Administrator's Garden and Lingering Garden are fine examples.

But now that domestic tourism has taken off in China, the former private gardens are no longer the tranquil retreats they were designed to be. Local sightseers flock to their favourite scenic corners to spend happy hours photographing each other. Still, the gardens have a unique charm, as does the small city of Suzhou itself, with its busy bridges and canals, narrow avenues of plane trees and peeling, white-washed homes.

To get there, you can hire a car and driver from your hotel, but the train ride is easy, more adventurous and cheaper. Book a first or 'soft' class ticket a day in advance at CITS (see page 23). Trains to Suzhou are frequent, with the first leaving before 6 am, but although there are several trains returning to Shanghai each day there is a risk you might not be able to return to Shanghai on the same day.

Suzhou canal

CITS offers a one day Suzhou tour by 'Panda' bus. Guide services, admission charges and lunch are all included and the bus, which operates three times a week, makes pick-ups from various Shanghai hotels.

Suzhou certainly warrants an overnight stay in order to get the feel of this place and to see some of the things that lend the place its reputation throughout China. Suitable hotels include the Lee Gardens managed **Bamboo Grove Hotel** (108 Zhu Hui Lu; tel. 520-5601; US$100 upwards), the **Suzhou Hotel** (115 Shi Quan Lu; tel. 522-4646; US$70 upwards) and the **Nan Yuan Guest House** (249 Shi Quan Lu; tel. 522-7661; US$50 upwards).

■ WUXI

Wuxi, which literally means 'without tin', is an interesting city about two hours train journey from Shanghai. Originally, the city was named Youxi—'with tin'—but supplies were eventually depleted during the Han Dynasty (206 BC–220 AD) and so the name needed to be changed. Less touristed than Suzhou, the city offers picturesque canal scenery (try the Nan Chang Lu), numerous markets and a beautiful resort area around the large freshwater Lake Tai—one of China's five largest lakes. Like Suzhou, Wuxi remains an important centre for the production of silk. A visit to one of the silk-spinning factories can be arranged through Wuxi CITS (tel. 270-5864). Today, Wuxi is known for high-technology products and light industry.

The **Pan Pacific Wuxi Grand Hotel** (tel. 670-6789; rooms from US$90) offers a four star standard, thought the more modest **Hubin** (tel. 670-1888) and **Sunshine** (tel. 670-2771) are very friendly hotels with prime lakeside locations. Boat excursions can be arranged to take in some of the islands on the lake. Furthermore, a cruise along the Grand Canal to Suzhou on a tourist boat (taking around four hours) is an unforgettable experience. The sides of the canal are lined with factories and warehouses obscuring the rice-paddies and fish-ponds behind. But it is the frenetic activity on the water—the convoys of heavily laden barges and endless smiles from the boat families—that makes the journey a real highlight for many travellers. This trip can also be arranged by CITS.

The Jewish Legacy Of Shanghai

Tess Johnston

Scholars debate when Jews first came to China, but it is certain that a Jewish community existed in Kaifeng during the Song Dynasty (12th century) and that the practice of Judaism by Chinese Jews had died out in China by the middle of the 19th century.

Beginning in the 1840s, Jews from Baghdad (including the Sassoons and Kadoories) came to Shanghai to live and engage in trade. The Russian Revolution of 1917 set off the first major wave of modern Jewish emigration to China, with the Jewish community in Harbin reaching 10,000, while others settled in Tianjin and Shanghai, the freest free port of all, where no passport was required for residence.

The rise of Nazism in Germany precipitated the second diaspora, from 1933 to 1941, with well-educated German and Austrian Jews migrating mostly to Shanghai, where they built synagogues and established a thriving Jewish community. In 1939 there were 20,000 Jews in Shanghai, 3,000 in Harbin and 2,000 in Tianjin. Almost all of these Jews left China after 1949, and at present the few who remain are employed by the Chinese government.

Shanghai has had seven synagogues over the course of the last century. Of these, Ohel Rachel (Shanxi Bei Lu) is now occupied by the Shanghai Education Bureau; Ohel Moishe (62 Changyang Lu) is partially demolished and partially occupied by the Shanghai Mental Hospital; New Synagogue (Xiangyang Nan Lu, near Huaihai Zhong Lu) is the auditorium of the Shanghai Education College; and the Shearith Israel (probably 541 Dong Daming Lu) is partly demolished and has been incorporated into residences.

There were four Jewish cemeteries, all of which have been demolished. All the cemeteries in Shanghai containing foreign graves were destroyed and ploughed under during the height of the Cultural Revolution. Only Sassoon's grave now remains intact.

The Shanghai Jewish Hospital (83 Fenyang Lu) is now the Shanghai Ear, Nose and Throat Hospital. The former Jewish Club (20 Fenyang Lu) houses the Shanghai Conservatory of Music. The Jewish Recreational Club (formerly 35 Moulmein Road, today Maoming Bei Lu) has been converted into private residences. And the Kadoorie Mansion, known as the Marble House (64 Yanan Xi Lu), which for a time served as the headquarters for the Jewish Club, is today one of Shanghai's Children's Palaces.

Doing Business In Shanghai

May it be permitted to a traveller to remark that if men were to give to the learning of Chinese and of Chinese requirements and methods of business a little of the time which is lavished on sport and other amusements, there might possibly be less occasion for the complaint that large fortunes are no longer to be made in Chinese business.

For indeed, from ignorance of the language and reliance on that limited and abominable vocabulary known as 'Pidgin', the British merchant must be more absolutely dependent on his Chinese compradore than he would care to be at home on his confidential clerk. Even in such lordly institutions as the British banks on the Bund it seems impossible to transact even such a simple affair as cashing a cheque without calling in the aid of a sleek, supercilious-looking, richly-dressed Chinese, a shroff or compradore, who looks as if he knew the business of the bank and were capable of running it. It is different at the Yokohama Specie Bank, which has found a footing in Shanghai, in which the alert Japanese clerks manage their own affairs and speak Chinese. May I be forgiven?

Isabella Bird, *The Yangtse River and Beyond* (1899)

The People's Republic of China is wrestling with the immense complexities of transforming a backward agricultural economy into a technologically advanced industrial society capable, within the early decades of the next century, of providing what most of its people would now consider prosperity. It is aspiring, in other words, to leap from the Middle Ages to the 21st century.

The transformation, begun in the late 1970s, has involved the country in wave after wave of economic reforms aimed at converting it from a centralized Soviet-style economy into something less controlled and more outgoing. In the countryside, communes have been replaced by private farming and cottage industries; and in the cities, capitalist styles of management and finance have been introduced. The involvement of the Western world, for so long kept at arm's length, is now seen to be essential, and a string of coastal cities have been opened up to foreign trade and investment. China needs not only new technology to replace the old, but also the know-how that goes with modern hardware and management.

Seeing China as the world's last great developing market, many Western investors have come to do business with the Chinese. Some have found themselves chasing unrealistic objectives; others have been more successful. All have learnt that it takes great patience and a large amount of effort to gain a foothold in China. The China market is extremely complex, and Western firms may need to deal with several bureaux of several ministries before they can even begin to negotiate. Besides, the

Nanpu Bridge, over the Huangpu River

Chinese have little foreign exchange to spare and prefer to do business with companies that can give them access to low-cost loans and international markets for their exports. The most successful companies will be those that can incorporate these objectives in their approach to China.

For a century, Shanghai was China's gateway to the world. On the eve of the Communist takeover in 1949, the city not only accounted for a fifth of the country's total industrial output, it was also the funnel for some two-thirds of China's foreign trade. Over the next four decades, however, it lost its lead, with its contribution to national industrial output plunging to 6% and its share of exports falling to below a tenth of total receipts in 1990. It attracted much less foreign investment than, say, Guangdong, and its annual economic growth lagged well behind that of the booming southern province.

However, the city's fortune was to change with the turn of the 1990s, and with the backing of the nations patriarch, Deng Xiaoping, Shanghai's reform programmes hit a new note in 1992. Since then there has been a frenzy of development and the Mayor of Shanghai, Huang Ju, has disclosed plans to transform the city into an international economic, finance and trade city by 2010. An important role in the global economy is envisaged for Shanghai. The city has already surpassed the Special Economic Zones of south China in its move towards an international market system.

Yet even though the doors are open the massive speculative activity christened in Shanghai is not unleashed. Beijing, which takes 60% of Shanghai's tax revenue, remains very sensitive to the pace and direction of change; and from the international business viewpoint there is no fast lane if China sticks to the grand socialist market economy. The transition from a centrally organized economy to a socialist market economy, and beyond to a full market system is fraught with ideological, political and economic difficulties.

Though the mayor has recently promised to develop markets, reduce bureaucratic intrusion and broaden the range of markets for foreign investment, the state has the final say—foreign business concerns are bound by the Chinese system.

For the visitor, the effects of the recent reforms are apparent all over the city. Shanghai has embarked upon a series of urban reconstruction projects, which include the total renewal of the city's infrastructure, the development of modern new commercial, cultural and trade areas, as well as massive housing projects which will move the old city population to the suburbs. To the end of 1994 over US$6 billion was invested in infrastructure projects and something like US$100 billion will be required to complete development plans for the city by the year 2000.

A new airport is planned for the Pudong New Area which will have five times the handling capacity of the present Hongqiao Airport—up to 100 million passengers a year. The four runway and US$10 billion airport should be open by the year 2000, though final completion is expected in 2015. Super-highways connecting Shanghai to Hangzhou and the Nanjing, the capital of Jiangsu Province, are also to be realized.

Capital has been forthcoming from the Asian Development and the World Bank; though the future success of the city's redevelopment projects will rely on huge injections of foreign capital which will only be realised if the central government relaxes its fiscal regulations.

Between 1991 and 1993 foreign investment in Shanghai surpassed the total of the preceding 30 years. In 1994 alone some US$10 billion of foreign capital entered the city. Most foreigners doing business in Shanghai do so in conjunction with a Chinese partner. Such joint-venture companies, previously limited to export-led activities can now gain a foothold in the burgeoning domestic market. As an example, Shanghai's department stores brightly display Chinese-manufactured international brand named household electrical items and toiletries. Joint-ventures account for around 20% of the city's total sales revenue. Permission to form wholly owned ventures is granted primarily to top priority hi-tech export-orientated projects.

In Shanghai, joint-ventures are largely confined to automobile production, chemicals, steel, power equipment, household electrical appliances and telecommunications. Many restrictions remain for foreign investors in Shanghai. Foreign firms are looking to the future in the hope of expanding their operations and waiting to see what opportunities will present themselves in the Pudong New Area. There are now around 150 multi-national companies with interests in Shanghai. As for smaller foreign investments over 3500 new joint and wholly owned ventures were approved by the city government in 1993 alone.

Obstacles to the foreign investor, apart from political and cultural intransigence, include sky-high rents (higher than Manhattan!), congestion, staffing difficulties and limited access to the money and securities market, making it difficult to initiate and even more difficult to develop their business in the manner many would like.

As a case in point, with a relaxation of regulations in 1991 over 30 commercial banks have now established offices in Shanghai. However their role is severely limited by the fact that they can only deal in foreign currency and are excluded from the domestic Rmb market. The banks' future success is dependent on the liberation of the financial sector; which the Bank of China has stated an intention to reform in the near future.

Similarly on the Shanghai Stock Exchange, foreigners are presently restricted to trade in B shares, with A shares firmly in the domestic domain. Again a declared intention has been made to allow foreigners free trade in the future. The Shanghai Stock Exchange, established in 1990, was capitalized at around US$30 billion in 1994. The state has been propping up the market following a slump in 1993 and foreigners are critical of insider trading and market manipulation. Originally set up

The Rape Of The Lock

My barber begins to cut with extreme caution, almost one hair at a time. Sometimes I feel as though he is just snipping the scissors above my head, vamping until he gets a clear notion of how to treat this uncharted territory. My hair is thick, blond and long. It is also dirty.

"Not many foreigners come in here," he finally says as he pecks around my ears, seeming to beg the question of what he should do with the ruin of hair on my head.

"Just cut a lot off, however you want to," I say.

He is not pleased with these instructions. Actually, I am tired of my longish (by Chinese standards) hair, and I am curious to see what the Chinese notion of a Western haircut is. I am not anxious to give detailed instructions. I do not really care what the outcome looks like, as long as it does not alarm the Chinese for the next month.

The person immediately adjacent to me is a young man in his twenties. He has almost finished, and it is clear that he has some Shanghai style-consciousness. (Before the Cultural Revolution, Shanghai evidenced much more concern for fashion than other parts of China.) His hair is shaped back on the sides like "fenders," and is held in place by some oil, an unheard-of outrage in Peking or the countryside. He has carefully coached the barber the whole time. He holds a hand mirror throughout so that he can have a view of what is happening on all sides. Although his vanity stands out here in Shanghai, The People's Republic of China, he would doubtless be considered a model of modesty and self-abnegation in most of the hair salons of the West. It's all a question of proportion.

My own barber has hit his pace now. He is onto something, although it is not yet evident what it will finally mean to my new demeanor. He keeps sweeping back the long hair on top of my head as he cuts, suggesting that he plans this posture to be its ultimate repose.

The manager suddenly charges at the door, snapping a towel as he goes. The mob of children scatters across the sidewalk in glee. There is a retarded child of about thirteen with them. He is not as agile as the others, and does not run. He just stands there in the middle of the sidewalk smiling a goofy smile. Some of the other children laugh and point at him, which almost sends him backing into a lit hibachi pot a woman is cooking on right out in the middle of the sidewalk. She swats him on the head with a wicker broom in a way which is only partially good-natured. The retarded child remains immobile, and gives her his goofy smile. The other children laugh mirthfully.

Back inside, my head is taking shape. The barber has definitely decided on the swept-back look; the Janos Misczek Czech freedom fighter of 1957 special! Early Toscanini!

I nod approval, and he squires me over to the wash basin, where he shampoos my head. Then he gives me a shave. He shaves my forehead, nose, ears, as well as my cheeks and chin. I feel like the kind of inordinately hairy foreigner described in the days of yore by Chinese who first encountered Westerners.

He gets out the hair drier, sweeps my hair back resolutely on top, and begins to dry it in place. He has lost all timidity now, and is wantonly shaping it and patting it with his free hand as he dries. It acquires a springy puffed-up quality, as though the hair had been immobilized in place by some magnetic force.

He places hot towels on my face. They feel wonderful.

I'm done.

I pay 25 yuan, shake hands, and leave through the sea of children at the door, who hastily part as if I were Moses.

I walk down P'ing t'ien lu past one of the more stately mansions of the old French Concession. I catch a profile of my new hairdo in a shop window.

I am transformed.

Orville Schell, *In the People's Republic*

Suggested Sightseeing Itinerary

The following itinerary of six kilometres (3.7 miles) will take an entire day, including lunch. The itinerary can be taken by taxi but is difficult to accomplish by bicycle, as several of the streets are closed to bikes.

Begin at the parking lot in front of **Lao Fandian** in the heart of the Old Town. Explore the twisting lanes and shops that lead you to the **Bridge of Nine Turnings** and the **Huxinting Teahouse**, and visit the **Yu Garden**.

From there head north to Renmin Lu, west to Henan Lu, and north on Henan Lu to Guangdong Lu, turn right (east) to Nos 218–228 and browse in the **Shanghai Antique and Curio Store**.

Continue east to the Bund, turn left (north) and pay a quick visit to the **Dong Feng Hotel** and view the faded elegance of the **Shanghai Club** (resisting the urge to dive into **Kentucky Fried Chicken!**). Then pass the old **Hongkong and Shanghai Bank** building and the offices and hotels as far as **Waibaidu Bridge**. (Optional stop in the **Friendship Store**, or cross the bridge to see the site of the **Stock Exchange** in the **Pujiang Hotel**.)

Go back down the **Bund** to the **Peace Hotel** at the corner of Nanjing Dong Lu. Look around the ground floor and take lunch in the richly decorated eighth floor restaurant overlooking the river. Take a peep at the old ballroom on the same floor.

Walk off lunch by heading west along Nanjing Lu as far as the **Park Hotel**. Depending on how much window and actual shopping you do, this

in 1992, Shanghai at present has eight separate commodities exchanges.

Many of the joint-ventures and multi-national companies are found in one of several development sites around Shanghai, as manufacturing has been increasingly dispersed to suburban districts, where special economic and industrial zones and satellite towns have been built.

■ HONGQIAO ECONOMIC AND TECHNOLOGICAL DEVELOPMENT ZONE
The Shanghai Municipal Government decided to build the zone in 1982 to attract foreign capital, clearing more than 500 homes and 20 factories to make room for it. The 66-hectare (163-acre) area lies between the city centre and Hongqiao International Airport. The zone contains consulate buildings, offices, high-rise apartment blocks and recreational facilities as well as several joint-venture hotels. Banking, customs, commodity inspection, insurance and courier services are available in the zone. Hongqiao is very popular with foreign investors and is a preferred location for

will take from 40 minutes to infinity (probably the latter!).

Continue on Nanjing Lu past **People's Park** (formerly the racecourse), passing the old **Race Club** building with its tall clock tower. Take a break in the park, if you want to get away from it all.

End the journey here, or continue west on Nanjing Xi Lu to Changshu Lu, where a left (south) turn takes you to **Marble House** (now a Children's Palace) and the **Hilton** and **Equatorial** hotels.

For a second day, add the **Jade Buddha Temple** and the residence of either Soong Ching-ling or Sun Yat-sen in the morning. Take the slow and relaxing **Huangpu River Cruise** in the afternoon, or a quicker local ferry across the Huangpu: the return journey should take no longer than about 30 minutes. Spend the late afternoon in a coffee shop on the Nanjing Dong Lu or in the **Peace Hotel**; or at the pub/brewery to the side of the old **Customs House**. As many of the big stores stay open until 10 pm catch up on a little shopping either before or after dinner (or both!). If you have the energy spend the remainder of the evening dancing to the Peace Hotel jazz band.

On day three, one might visit the **Lu Xun Museum and former Residence** in **Hongkou Park**. Perhaps the best way to say farewell to Shanghai is to view the city from the top of one of the taller hotels, where one might enjoy a fine meal: the Hilton, Park, Shanghai Mansions, Garden Hotel and Jinjiang Tower all offer a grand panorama day and night.

many Shanghai government departments. Its status as a major finance and business centre will be enhanced with the completion of the Metro Line Number Two in 1997 and of the 'Shanghai Plaza' development which is presently under construction. Due to be completed in 1998, the 8 billion Rmb edifice will house five office towers, exhibition venues, apartment blocks, entertainment and shopping complexes as well as a five star hotel. The corporation responsible for the development and management of the zone is the Shanghai Hongqiao United Development Co Ltd (SHUDC).

■ HI-TECH PARKS

Caohejing is 11 kilometres (7 miles) from the city centre. It was laid out for research institutes and plants specializing in computers, large-scale integrated circuits, optical fibre communications, microelectronics, precision instruments, bioengineering, robotics and space technology. Currently there are 116 joint-ventures, 40 state enterprises and 130 domestic private businesses in the area. Approved in 1994, there is a three stage plan to transform the area into a hi-tech commercial city which is expected to account for 10% of Shanghai's GDP by the year 2000. There are smaller parks at Zhangjiang in Pudong and at Shanghai University. A China International Textile Technology Development Zone has also been created.

■ MINHANG ECONOMIC AND TECHNOLOGICAL DEVELOPMENT ZONE
A manufacturing estate to the south of the city proper, Minhang is where Shanghai's power equipment industries are concentrated. The majority of projects located in the zone are export-oriented or involve advanced technology. Among the joint-ventures established here are Xerox of Shanghai, Braun Electric, Squibb Pharmaceuticals Ltd, and Shanghai-Hong Kong Universal Toys Ltd. Minhang covers over two square kilometres (526 acres) and is run by the Shanghai Minhang United Development Co Ltd.

■ SHANGHAI FOREIGN INVESTMENT COMMISSION (SFIC)
This organization was formed in 1988 to examine and approve foreign investment projects valued at between US$5 million and US$30 million. Those projects not falling within its brief must be referred to Beijing. Besides the examination and approval of project proposals, SFIC is responsible for providing information to prospective investors, making recommendations of possible partners, and offering various consultancy services in the matter of laws, policies and regulations. It will also help with any problems encountered by the foreign investor during the initial stages of operation.

■ PUDONG NEW AREA
Until the early 1990s Pudong was a barren, neglected landscape occupied by fields, dilapidated factories and warehouses. It wasn't Shanghai—very few city people went there and its residents coming to the city to work chugged home on the overcrowded ferry. Today the Oriental Pearl TV Tower, Shanghai's new landmark dominates the skyline, but by the year 2000 the skyline is likely to resemble Hong Kong or New York and the TV tower won't look so misplaced.

Pudong is destined to become the new Shanghai, a futuristic metropolis likely to be inspired by designs from international architects reflecting its intent to become a truly international city. Work so far has concentrated on infrastructural development, with the upward physical development accelerating from 1995 onwards to the millennium and beyond. Apart from the existing and planned tunnels and bridges, 16 more ferries are to ply the Huangpu and Pudong will have the terminal of Metro Line Number Two. In Pudong itself there are plans for a new railway system, more than 30 10,000 ton berths and a new airport. Increased accessibility has already pushed property prices up to match international levels.

The Pudong New Area has four main development zones: the Lujiazui Finance and Trade Zone, the Jingqiao Export Processing Zone, the Waigaoqiao Free Trade Zone and the Zhangjiang Hi-tech Zone. Pudong is focusing on the service industries, including trade and finance, and the government is offering tax benefits and other preferential policies to lure foreign investment. Nearly half of all foreign enterprises are presently located in the Waigaoqiao area, which has seen exports increase 20-fold between 1992 and 1994.

One area has been specifically set aside for tourism development: the Huaxia Tourism Development Zone will include country clubs, villas and amusement parks. In the Lujiazui Zone there are plans to build Asia's tallest building—a Sino-Japanese-American joint-venture. The 90-storey building should be completed by the year 2000.

■ SUBURBAN AREAS

Various counties are courting foreign investment, with industrial parks having been set up in Fengxian, Qingpu, Chongming, Jinshan, Nanhui and Songjiang. Over 600 foreign enterprises have moved to these areas; with names like Nestlé, Kenwood and Minolta to be found at Songjiang.

■ CONFERENCE AND EXHIBITION FACILITIES

Shanghai is fast becoming an international convention and exhibition centre with facilities provided at the Shanghai Exhibition Centre, the Shanghai Film Art Centre, the International Exhibition Centre (INTEX). The Shanghai Business Centre and theShanghai International Trade Centre. (Refer to Useful Addresses on page 156)

(Overleaf) View across Suzhou Creek

Recommended Reading

Much of the most fascinating reading material on Shanghai covers the period of the foreign concessions before 1949. Most of the books are out of print but are worth looking for in libraries or second-hand book shops. G Miller's *Shanghai: the Paradise of Adventurers* (Orsay 1937), written under a pseudonym by an American diplomat, was one of the best-known books on pre-1949 Shanghai. *Shanghai: A Handbook for Travellers and Residents* (Kelly and Walsh 1920), is an interesting period guidebook by the Reverend Charles Darwent. *All About Shanghai and Environs*, an illustrated guide brought out in Shanghai in 1934–35, has been re-issued by Oxford University Press (1983) and is well worth reading. Other recent guidebooks include *Shanghai Rediscovered* by Christopher Knowles (Lascelles 1990) and *Shanghai Info Guide* (Far East Media Ltd, Info Guide 1989).

For a history of Shanghai from its earliest days there is *Yellow Creek: the Story of Shanghai* by J V Davidson-Houston (Putman 1962); and Betty Peh-T'i Wei's scholarly *Shanghai, Crucible of Modern China* (Oxford University Press 1990). Translated excerpts from Chinese novels dealing with the life of Shanghai's singsong girls are collected in *Chinese Middle-brow Fiction* edited by Liu Ts'un-yan (Chinese University Press, Hong Kong 1984). For an overall view of Shanghai's past by an aficionado, there is Pan Ling's *In Search of Old Shanghai* (Joint Publishing Company 1982), a short but very useful companion to a guide of Shanghai. Pan Ling, who now writes as Lynn Pan, is also the author of *Old Shanghai: Gangsters in Paradise* (Heinemann Asia 1984), a reconstruction of the life and times of Du Yuesheng, Shanghai's legendary secret-society chief and mobster.

A portrait of Shanghai in the late 1920s is to be found in André Malraux's *Man's Estate* (Penguin 1961), first published in French in 1933 as *La Condition Humaine*. In the same year Chinese writer Mao Dun published his great novel set in Shanghai, *Midnight* (Beijing Foreign Languages Press 1979). Sterling Seagrave's *The Soong Dynasty* (Harper & Row 1985) is full of riveting detail on that most extraordinary of Shanghai families. No novel peopled by pre-1949 Shanghai characters is funnier and wiser than *Wei Cheng* by Qian Zhongshu, which is available in an English translation entitled *Fortress Besieged* by Jeanne Kelly and Nathan K Mao (Indiana University Press 1979). Vicki Baum's *Shanghai '37*, a novel on the city at the start of the Sino-Japanese War, is available in paperback edition (Oxford University Press 1986). The cloak-and-dagger of 1930s Shanghai is wonderfully caught in the comic *The Blue Lotus*, one of *The Adventures of Tintin* series of books by Hergé (English translation by L Lonsdale-Cooper and Michael Turner, Magnet paperback, Methuen Children's

Books Ltd). Harriet Sergeant documents the 1920s and 1930s from a largely foreign perspective in *Shanghai* (Jonathan Cape 1991). A recollection of Shanghai from the 1920s to the 1950s is *Last Moments of a World* by Margaret Gaan (Norton 1981). Peter Hibbard's forthcoming book, *Peace at the Cathay*, views Shanghai society from the perspective of the Cathay Hotel and includes impressive illustrations.

Shanghai during wartime is described in three books: Noel Barber's *The Fall of Shanghai: The Communist Takeover in 1949* (Macmillan 1979), which draws extensively on interviews with people who lived through the period, is highly readable. Lawrence Earl's *Yangtze Incident* focuses on the adventures of the British frigate HMS *Amethyst* during the takeover. J G Ballard's novel about Longhua Camp, *Empire of the Sun* (Grafton Books 1985), powerfully evokes life in Shanghai during the Japanese occupation. (There is a film version of this novel directed by Steven Spielberg.)

The period of the Cultural Revolution is covered in Neil Hunter's *Shanghai Journal: an Eyewitness Account of the Cultural Revolution* (Praeger 1969, re-issued by OUP 1988). For what those years meant to one Shanghai inhabitant, a strong, courageous woman incarcerated in one of the city's prisons during the height of the Cultural Revolution, read Nien Cheng's gripping and incisive account of *Life and Death in Shanghai* (Grafton Books 1986). Anchee Min's *Red Azalea: Life and Love in China* (Victor Gollancz 1993) is an intensely moving, sensual and quite different kind of autobiography of a model member of the Red Guard who has to endure the harsh conditions of the communal farm and who is then plucked by one of Madame Mao's associates to become a star of the Chinese propaganda film industry in Shanghai.

Panda Books and Shanghai Literature have produced numerous translations of famous Chinese literature, including Cheng Naishan's *The Song Mother Taught Me to Sing*; and Lu Xing'er's collections of short stories, whose protagonists are women from all walks of life. Both these authors were born in Shanghai during the 1940s. It is also very worthwhile reading the prose and poetry of Lu Xun for clear accounts of the Chinese society he understood so well and for more personal and poetic insights into his fascinating sensibility.

Orville Schell's *Mandate of Heaven* (Simon & Schuster 1994) is an absorbing view of China's (and surely Shanghai's...) future with its new generation of entrepreneurs, dissidents, bohemians and technocrats (see Literary Extract, page 165).

An excellent photographic account of Shanghai during the Chinese Revolution is *Shanghai 1949: The End of an Era* (B T Batsford Ltd 1981), with photographs by Sam Tata and text by Ian McLacklan. Other photo-based accounts worth looking at are *Survey of Shanghai 1840s–1940s* (Shanghai People's Fine Arts Publishing House, 1993) which comes with an English supplement, and *A Last Look: Western Architecture in Old Shanghai* (Old China Hand Press 1993) by Tess Johnston and Deke Erh.

Advertisement for The Cathay Hotel

Visions Of Cathay

Peter Hibbard

Like an Art Deco rocket ship arising from the impassioned waters of the Huangpu River, the Cathay Hotel of the Thirties was a powerful symbol of thrusting Shanghai society. Sleek and elegant, modest in outward adornment, rich and extravagant in its heart, the mood of Shanghai exuded from its walls. All who wandered its corridors or came to rest within its chambers found an intimate friend.

The Cathay was much more than a social institution. It was the body of Shanghai, an anchor of stability and familiarity and a Ferris wheel of novelty and surprise. A sublime mélange of fantasy and reality, the hotel embodied a vision of the future, while housing the best of the past.

The building is an important urban landmark, which today finds itself printed on a handkerchief draped across the face of an awakening metropolis. As the north building of the Peace Hotel, the former personality and richness of the Cathay has been lost, though many of the hotel's

The Peace Hotel

original features and fittings still survive—more have been replicated or remoulded. The hotel remains a must on any tourist itinerary. It's a great place to sit, sip a cocktail and conjure up images of the whirling Thirties.

A personal vision of the influential Sir Victor Sassoon, the Cathay Hotel was designed by Messrs. Palmer and Turner and opened for business in August 1929. Sceptics foretold failure, arguing that Shanghai already had an over-supply of hotel rooms or that it was too lavish and expensive. They proved to be wrong. The management had set out to make the Cathay Hotel the 'Claridges of the Far East'—and that they did!

Almost from its spectacular opening night the Cathay became Shanghai's premier rendezvous. It was the pace-setter, a monument to the marriage of art and technology, brimming with the very latest amenities and luxuries. Palatially furnished in imitated period and modern styles, the Cathay was practically built around an arsenal of fashionable Lalique lights.

Situated at one of the busiest intersections in Shanghai the Cathay provided a peaceful haven from the rush, clamour and heat of city life. The calmness and dignity was reflected in the decor and furnishings. No gaudy colours, no coarse ornaments, just quiet unobtrusive luxury, marble, bronze, velvet and tapestry. Likewise, the cosmopolitan clientele always shopped at the best shops and knew all the Right People. The Cathay was the Princess of Shanghai hotels.

The Cathay originally had nine suites de luxe, depicting a variety of national and historical styles with uncompromising luxury. There were two English suites, one contemporary and one Georgian in style. An Indian suite with filigree plaster work on the walls and ceilings was littered with rich coloured Indian carpets. Reputed Chinese and Japanese craftsmen were employed to ensure that the suites accredited to their respective countries were resplendent to the finest detail.

Then, as now, the eighth floor was the main public area. Emerging from the lift, visitors passed through a landing speckled with Lalique glass into an upper lounge and reading and writing room with walls of panelled bird's-eye maple and teak. This area was remodelled in 1933, to make way for the new Grill Room—an architectural extravaganza in purely Chinese style. Most of the room's features, which still survive, were adopted from the Forbidden

City and are framed by lattice work over the windows incorporating the Chinese characters for long life and happiness.

Now known as the Dragon-Phoenix Hall, it remains a popular venue for lingering visitors seeking a panorama across the Bund.

The features and decor provided the 'four minute guests'—as round the world tourists of the Thirties were known—with their only taste of Chinese art and architectural style. The dragon assumes a central position in the design of the restaurant's ceiling panels. Being the chief figure of Chinese mythology with an ability to control the rains (symbolizing peace and prosperity) and a power to rise from earth to heaven the dragon came to represent the Emperor. The Empress is symbolized in the design through the figure of a phoenix. The ceiling panels were adopted from door panels in the Forbidden City. During the Cultural Revolution the staff managed to fit a false ceiling below to protect them from the savage vandalism of the Red Guards.

The other main feature of the eighth floor was the main dining room and ballroom, now known as the Peace Hall. Rose tinted curtains and carpets splashed with gold, dull silver and gold walls, white birch furniture, a white maple dance floor and a liberal show of Lalique lighting fused together to create one of the most beautiful dining rooms in the world. Sir Victor Sassoon had a passion for entertaining. The ballroom was often the setting for one of his eccentric fancy dress parties. It was transformed into a toy shop or a circus arena or whatever the theme of the party happened to be and crowded with respectable local figures making great fools of themselves.

Unfortunately, the great heyday of the Cathay was to be short-lived. Commencing with a bombing incident on 'Bloody Saturday' in 1937 the hotel's fortunes fell with those of the city. The parties continued, however, right up to the Japanese occupation of the hotel in late 1941. In the early Forties, lavish entertainment was seen as wasteful, so all proceeds from the Tower night-club went to the British war effort. After the war, the hotel played host to the American and British military, only to be usurped by the Nationalists and then to be made virtually redundant by the Communists.

Practical Information

Hotels

In recent years Shanghai has experienced a boom in hotel building resulting in an impressive range being on offer. There are numerous foreign-managed, modern hotels as well as many interesting old hotels, including converted residence blocks and walled villa estates.

The National Tourism Administration initiated a star-rating system for hotels in 1990—which roughly corresponds to international standards. This has forced many hotels to upgrade facilities. However, maintenance of service standards is still problematic, even for some of the better hotels. Little hotel development is planned for the area west of the Huangpu River, though the Peace Hotel is at present constructing a luxury west wing. Most future hotels, including a Shangri-La, will be built in the Pudong New Area.

Shanghai hotels are already the most expensive in China, and a service charge — usually of 15%—is added to the basic room rate. However some hotels offer special off-season, weekend or long-term rates.

With Shanghai's growing importance as an international centre of industry and commerce, many of the best Shanghai hotels can offer excellent facilities for meetings and exhibitions.

FIVE STAR HOTELS

Garden Hotel Shanghai
58 Maoming Nan Lu; tel. 415-1111; tlx 30157 GHSH CN; fax 415-8866
上海花园酒店　茂名南路58号
500 rooms, starting from US$200, suites from US$440. Chinese, Western and Japanese restaurants, business centre, health club, swimming pool, tennis courts, function rooms. Built on the site of the former Cercle Sportif Français (later more mundanely called the Jingjiang Club), architects have ingeniously incorporated some of the pre-1949 building into the ground floor and first floor of this new high-rise hotel. The magnificent oval ballroom, carefully restored to its former Art Deco splendour, is worth a visit. Opened in 1990. Run by the Japanese Group, Okura Hotels, this is one of the city's top hotels.

Jinjiang Tower
161 Changle Lu; tel. 433-4488; tlx 33652 FOJJT CN; fax 433-3265
新锦江大酒店　长乐路161号

640 rooms and suites, starting from US$180. Chinese and Western restaurants, business centre, swimming pool, health club, disco and function rooms. This striking cylindrical tower, fully opened in 1990, is the flagship of Shanghai's powerful Jinjiang Group. Set in the same complex as the older Jinjiang hotel buildings, the Tower has all the facilities of a top-class international hotel. Service, however, still has elements of old-style local Chinese management.

Portman Shangri-La
1376 Nanjing Xi Lu; tel. 279-8888; tlx 33272 PSH CN; fax 279-8899
波特曼香格里拉酒店　南京西路1376号
647 rooms and suites, starting from US$215 and US$600 respectively. Four restaurants, swimming pool, health club, squash, racquetball, tennis, lawn bowls, business centre, function rooms, exhibition centre, theatre. Part of the impressive Shanghai Centre, designed by American group John Portman and Associates, this is one of Shanghai's most striking new hotels. Conveniently located on Nanjing Xi Lu, it is flanked by office and residential apartment blocks housing the bulk of Shanghai's foreign businessmen and expatriates. The ambitious interior contains a range of impressive works of art. Managed by Shangri-La Hotels International.

Shanghai Hilton International
250 Hua Shan Lu; tel. 248-0000; tlx 33612 HILTL CN; fax 248-3848
上海静安希尔顿酒店　华山路250号
800 rooms, starting from US$235, suites from US$350. Eight cafés, restaurants and bars. Delectable cakes and pastries from lobby bakery counter. Grand ballroom and function rooms, swimming pool, health club, tennis and squash courts, business centre. Executive floor with concierge and butler. One of Shanghai's best hotels, the Hilton is conveniently situated between the city's established commercial districts and the new development zone, Hongqiao. Besides the Atrium Café—a most attractive coffee shop with natural lighting and garden setting—the hotel also offers Sichuanese, Cantonese, Shanghainese and Japanese cuisine in its restaurants.

Shanghai JC Mandarin
1225 Nanjing Xi Lu; tel. 279-1888; tlx 33939 SJCMH CN; fax 279-1822
上海锦沧文华大酒店　南京西路1225号
Over 500 rooms, starting from US$200, suites from US$380. Chinese and Western restaurants, business centre, swimming pool, health club, tennis and squash courts, function rooms. A fine-looking hotel, opened mid-1990, well located on Nanjing Xi Lu, opposite the Shanghai Centre with an efficient management from Singaporean group, Singapore Mandarin. One of Shanghai's best hotels.

Sheraton Hua Ting

1200 Caoxi Bei Lu; tel. 439-1000; tlx 33589 SHHTH CN; fax 255-0830

华亭喜来登宾馆　漕溪北路1200号

1,008 rooms, 40 suites. Rooms from US$170, suites from US$250. Coffee shop, French, Italian and Chinese restaurants, disco, swimming pool, bowling alley, tennis court, health club and gymnasium, billiards, business centre. Large ballroom and function rooms. The first hotel in Shanghai to be managed by an international chain, the Sheraton is housed in an enormous S-shaped building with two exterior glass elevators. Facilities are comprehensive and include the hotel's own fleet of taxis and a shuttle service to the airport. The hotel is located in the southwest of the city.

The Westin Shanghai

5 Zunyi Nan Lu; tel. 275-8888; tlx 33345 PASHC CN; fax 275-5420

上海威斯汀大饭店　遵叉南路5号

578 rooms, starting from US$200, suites from US$275. Chinese, Western and Japanese restaurants, business centre, health club, function rooms. Opened at the end of 1990 this attractive hotel, under Western management, is considered to be the top quality hotel in the new Hongqiao development zone. Fifteen minutes from downtown.

Four Star Hotels
Galaxy Hotel

888 Zhongshan Xi Lu; tel. 275-8888; tlx 33176 SGHRD CN; fax 275-0201

银河宾馆　中山西路888号

673 rooms, starting from US$120, suites from US$220. Apartments also available. Located in the Hongqiao development zone 7 km from the airport. Chinese, Western and Korean restaurants, bowling alley and health club. The Gallery Club, open until 4 am is one of the most popular disco venues in the city.

Holiday Inn Crowne Plaza (Yin Xing)

388 Pan Yu Lu; tel. 252-8888; 30310 SFAC CN; fax 252-8545

上海银星皇冠假日酒店　番禺路388号

534 rooms, starting from US$170, suites from US$388. In the old French Concession, 9 km from the airport. Business centre, health club, indoor swimming pool, squash courts, Western and Chinese restaurants, karaoke and disco, beauty salon, medical services, adjacent film centre (five theatres).

Hotel Equatorial

65 Yanan Xi Lu; tel. 248-1688; tlx 33188 EQUAT CN; fax 248-4033

上海贵都酒店　延安西路65号
526 rooms, starting from US$180, suites from US$280. Popular with business travellers, the hotel features French and Japanese, as well as Chinese, cuisine. It offers excellent sports and recreational facilities for hotel guests and subscribers to the hotel based Shanghai International Club.

Hotel Sofitel Hyland Shanghai

505 Nanjing Xi Lu; tel. 351-5888; tlx 30386 SHLSO CN; fax 351-4088
海仑宾馆　南京西路505号
389 rooms, starting from US$160, suites from US$260. Located right in the heart of Nanjing Lu, this impressive new hotel offers a world of dining and entertainment, with Shanghainese, Cantonese and French cuisine. Managed by the French Accor Corporation.

Jianguo Hotel

439 Caoxi Bei Lu; tel. 439-9299; tlx 33951 JGH CN; fax 439-9714
上海建国宾馆　漕溪北路439号
464 rooms, starting from US$110, suites from US$260. Located in the rapidly developing area of the western suburbs, close to Xujiahui Cathedral and the new luxury department stores. Western and Chinese restaurants, disco and karaoke. Popular with European tour groups. Local management.

Jinjiang Hotel

59 Maoming Nan Lu; tel. 258-2582; tlx 33380 BCJJH CN; fax 472-5588
锦江饭店　茂名南路59号
700 rooms, starting from US$140, suites from US$220. 14 restaurants, shopping arcade (including bookstore and supermarket), disco, health club. Originally a residential hotel complex set in the heart of the French Concession, the hotel's oldest building—the north block—was known as the Cathay Mansions, dating from 1929. It was at the Jinjiang that Premier Zhou Enlai and President Nixon completed the historic Shanghai Communique in February 1972, opening the way for China's reentry into the world community. Under local management.

Nikko Longbai

2451 Hongqiao Lu; tel. 268-9111; tlx 30138 NHISH CN; fax 268-9333
上海日航龙柏饭店　虹桥路2451号
390 rooms, starting from US$160, 32 suites from US$280. Swimming pool, tennis courts, health club, business centre, disco, Japanese, Continental and Chinese restaurants. Shuttle bus service to downtown and airport. This pleasant 11-storey hotel in a

spacious garden setting near to the airport is a favourite with many Japanese visitors. Among its excellent facilities are a particularly attractive coffee shop and a good Japanese restaurant. Managed by Nikko Hotels International.

Peace Hotel
20 Nanjing Dong Lu; tel. 321-1244; tlx 33914 BTHPH CN; fax 329-0300
和平饭店　南京东路20号
420 rooms in two wings, starting from US$95, suites from US$150. The former Cathay Hotel—the most outstanding Art Deco hotel of the Far East. Opened in 1929, and now incorporating the old Palace Hotel which dates from 1906. Work has now commenced on a new luxury wing on the Nanjing Dong Lu.

Rainbow Hotel
2000 Yanan Xi Lu; tel. 275-3388; tlx 30330 SRHF CN; fax 275-7244
虹桥迎宾馆　延安西路2000号
628 rooms, starting from US$115, suites from US$230. Chinese and Western restaurants, business centre, swimming pool, health club, karaoke, billiard, function rooms. This large new hotel in the Hongqiao development zone is already showing signs of wear. Locally managed, it caters to Taiwanese tour groups.

Shanghai Lan Sheng Hotel
1000 Quyang Lu; tel. 524-8000; tlx 33952 REGBC CN; fax 544-8400
上海兰生大酒店　曲阳路1000号
417 rooms, starting from US$135, suites from US$180. Located in the north of
Shanghai near Lu Xun Park, this modern hotel was previously called the Regal. Western and Chinese restaurants including a Food Street, health club, bowling and indoor
golf. A stately hotel with magnificently appointed bathrooms. Under Hong Kong
management.

Yangtze New World
2099 Yanan Xi Lu; tel. 275-0000; tlx 33675 YNWHR CN; fax 275-0750
上海扬子江大酒店　延安西路2099号
570 rooms, starting from US$160, suites from US$220. Five restaurants (Chinese and
Western), business centre, swimming pool, health club, disco and function rooms.
Opened mid-1990, this is a pleasant hotel run by the Hong Kong's New World Hotels
International. It is located in the Hongqiao development zone, on the airport road,
next to the Westin.

THREE STAR HOTELS
City Hotel Shanghai
5–7 Shanxi Nan Lu; tel. 255-1133; tlx 30031 SCH CN; fax 255-0211
上海城市酒店　陕西南路5-7号
257 rooms, starting from US$100, suites from US$180. Business centre, restaurants
for Cantonese, Sichuan and international cuisines, disco, swimming pool and gym.
An attractive silver and red skyscraper, this hotel opened in 1988 under Hong Kong
management.

Donghu Hotel
70 Donghu Road; tel. 415-8158; tlx 33453 BTHDH CN; fax 433-1275
东湖宾馆　东湖路70号
300 rooms, starting from US$85. Two restaurants with Chinese cuisine, swimming
pool, business centre, karaoke bar. Fifteen minutes to downtown. Until recently a
guesthouse for high-ranking Party cadres, the Donghu has been renovated and now
presents a somewhat mixed style, with modern furnishings and traditional furniture.
Building Number One was owned by Du Yuesheng, old Shanghai's most famous
gangster. Part of the hotel, a 10-bedroomed mansion at 7 Donghu Lu, is very evocative of 1930s Shanghai with its dark wood panelling, its decorated fireplaces, and its
stained glass windows. A group, or a family, can have the whole villa (also available
for long-term lets) for around US$100 per day.

Hengshan Hotel

534 Hengshan Lu; tel. 437-7050; tlx 33933 HSH CN; fax 433-5732

衡山宾馆　衡山路534号

232 rooms, starting from US$98, suites from US$165. Six restaurants, business centre, health club and billiards. Converted Art Deco apartment block (Picardie Mansions) now transformed into rooms with self-catering facilities. Short-term lets also available.

Hua Ting Guest House

2525 Zhongshan Xi Lu; tel. 481-3500; tlx 30192 HTGHS CN; fax 439-0322

华亭宾馆　中山西路2525号

189 rooms, starting from US$70, suites from US$120. Close to the Sheraton, the hotel has minimal facilities (one restaurant and business centre), but is conveniently located.

Jingan Hotel

370 Huashan Lu; tel. 248-1888; tlx 30022 BTHSC CN; fax 248-2657

静安宾馆　华山路370号

215 rooms, starting from US$110, suites from US$235. Three Chinese restaurants, one café serving Western food, business centre and a disco. Formerly the Haig Apartments, this quiet and comfortable guesthouse offers attentive service and good food. The modern west wing lacks the old-world atmosphere of the main block. The hotel's excellent bakery is a joint venture with a Hong Kong firm. Centrally located.

Jinjiang Pacific Hotel

104 Nanjing Xi Lu; tel. 327-6226; tlx 33909 BTHHF CN; fax 326-9620

锦江金门大酒店　南京西路104号

120 rooms, starting from US$60, suites from US$125. Opened as the China United Assurance Co. office and apartments in 1926, the hotel has recently dropped its former title as the Overseas Chinese Hotel. With its American designed Italian portico, it remains popular with overseas Chinese.

Jinjiang YMCA Hotel

123 Xizang Nan Lu; tel. 326-1040; tlx 33920 QNHSH CN; fax 320-1957

上海锦江青年会宾馆　西藏南路123号

154 rooms, starting from US$58, suites from US$118. Two restaurants, one Chinese and one Western. Additional facilities include a business centre, shopping arcade, gym and karaoke.

Jinsha Hotel

801 Jinshajiang Lu; tel. 257-8888; tlx 33454 BTHJD CN; fax 257-4149
金沙江大酒店　金沙江路801号
298 rooms, starting from US$55, suites from US$86. Seven restaurants, business centre, health club, disco and function room. Located in nondescript area northwest of the city. Its location and the difficulty of getting transport at short notice are a considerable drawback for businesspeople and individual travellers.

Longmen Hotel

777 Hengfeng Lu; tel. 317-000; tlx 33693 SLMHB CN; fax 317-2004
龙门宾馆　恒丰路777号
365 rooms, starting from US$80, suites from US$160. A modern hotel next to Shanghai Railway Station. Seven Chinese and Western restaurants, health centre, business centre, disco and karaoke. Local management.

Magnolia Hotel

1251 Siping Lu; tel. 545-6888; tlx 30331 MHR CN; fax 545-9499
白玉兰宾馆　四平路1251号
231 rooms, starting from US$60, suites from US$120. Large Chinese restaurant. Opened in July 1988, this middle-range hotel stands near Tongji University, northeast of Hongkou Park.

New Asia Hotel

422 Tiantong Lu; tel. 324-2210; 324-2210; tlx 30034 SNA CN; fax 399-9529
新亚大酒店　天潼路422号
304 rooms, starting from US$45, suites from US$120. Five Chinese restaurants and a French restaurant. Centrally located, the New Asia was built in 1934, and was previously run along the lines of Christian fellowship and healthy living.

Novotel Shanghai Yuan Lin

201 Baise Lu; tel. 470-1688; tlx 33680 SYLHR CN; fax 470-0007
上海诺富特园林宾馆　百色路201号
183 rooms, starting from US$80. Villas to let—minimum six months contract. Chinese and Western restaurants, business centre, health club, disco, tennis courts, function rooms. Located rather far out in the southwest of the city, this pleasant new hotel is run by the huge French management group, Accor. About forty minutes ride to downtown.

New Garden Hotel

1900 Hongqiao Lu; tel. 242-8577; tlx 33918 BTHNW CN; fax 242-3256

新苑宾馆　虹桥路1900号

324 rooms, starting from US$69. Seven Chinese restaurants, disco, business centre and shopping arcade. Located 4 km from the airport.

Ocean Hotel

1171 Dong Daming Lu; tel. 545-8888; tlx 30333 OCETL CN; fax 545-8993

远洋宾馆　东大名路1171号

347 rooms, starting from US$90, suites from US$180. Business centre, health club, disco, karaoke, shuttle bus service. Opened in 1989, run by a Hong Kong management company. Its 27th-floor restaurant is Shanghai's first revolving restaurant.

Park Hotel

170 Nanjing Xi Lu; tel. 327-5225; tlx 33932 PARK CN; fax. 327-6958

国际饭店　南京西路170号

208 rooms, starting from US$110, suites from US$180. The 22-storey Park was the tallest building between London and Tokyo when it opened in 1934. With an excellent location overlooking Renmin Park (the old racecourse), the Park played host to major nationalist figures in the old days. There are few reminders today of the hotel's past, but of its kind the Park remains one of Shanghai's most famous hotels.

Shanghai Hotel

505 Wulumuqi Bei Lu; tel. 248-0088; tlx 33295 SHR CN; fax 248-1056

上海宾馆　乌鲁木齐北路505号

551 rooms, starting from US$80, suites from US$160. Two Chinese and a Japanese restaurant. Operated by the Shanghai Tourism Bureau, this is a hotel which has to make little effort in order to compete for business. Tour groups are its speciality. Centrally located.

Shanghai International Airport Hotel

2550 Hongqiao Lu; tel. 268-8866; tlx 30033 SIAHA CN; fax 268-8393

上海国际机场宾馆　虹桥路2550号

308 rooms, starting from US$90, suites from US$160. Four restaurants (including Japanese), health club, function rooms. A pleasant hotel, opened in 1988, next to Hongqiao Airport. Japanese management.

Shanghai Mansions

20 Bei Suzhou Lu; tel. 324-6260; tlx 33921 SMB CN; fax 306-5147

上海大厦　北苏州路20号

246 rooms, starting from US$90, suites from US$115, This typical 1930s skyscraper commands a magnificent view from the north bank of Suzhou Creek, looking down along the waterfront and across the city. Opened in 1933, Broadway Mansions, as the 19-storey red-brick building was then called, was a smart residential hotel which at one time housed the US Military Advisory Group on the lower floors, with apartments for the foreign press above.

Swan Cindic Hotel

111 Jiangwan Lu, Hongkou; tel. 325-5255; tlx 30023 BTHSC CN; fax 324-8002

上海天鹅信谊宾馆　虹口区江湾路111号

191 rooms, starting from US$86, suites from US$128. Western and Chinese restaurants, business centre, disco. Pleasant interior despite unprepossessing tiled façade. Under local management, it is one of the few hotels located in northeast Shanghai, near the Lu Xun Park.

Tian Ma Hotel

471 Wuzhong Lu; tel. 242-5888; tlx 30901 BTHTM CN; fax 242-3149

天马大酒店　吴中路471号

199 rooms, starting from US$58, suites from US$168. Health club, billiards room, bowling alley, business centre. A new, locally run hotel with good facilities, including suites done up in national style (for example, the English Suite with electric log fireplace and hunting prints on the walls, and the Qing-Dynasty Suite with moon doorways and satin quilts). It is, however, inconveniently located down a long and potholed road in the western suburbs.

Windsor Evergreen Hotel

189 Baise Lu; tel. 470-0888; fax 470-4832

金岛温莎酒店　百色路189号

175 rooms, starting from US$80, suites from US$130. Opened in 1993 and located near the Botanical Gardens and Longhua Temple. Western and Chinese restaurants, business centre. Though in the far south of the city, the hotel shuttle bus connects various hotels in the downtown area. Hong Kong managed.

Two Star Hotels
Cherry Holiday Villa

77 Nonggong Lu (near the junction of Hongqiao Lu and Gubei Lu); tel. 275-8350; tlx 33908 BTHYH CN; fax 275-6457

樱花渡假村　农工路77号

WHEELBARROWS
SHANGHAI

132 rooms, starting from US$53, suites from US$88. Two restaurants, business centre and a disco. Villa-type hotel, consisting of several concrete buildings and a few swings and roundabouts. Reached at the end of a bumpy lane off the Hongqiao Road.

Metropole Hotel

180 Jiangxi Zhong Lu; tel. 321-3030; tlx 33947 SXCH CN; fax 321-7365

新城饭店　江西中路180号

140 rooms, starting from US$43, suites from US$80. Refurbished back in 1990, the Metropole dates from 1932. In the basement is the American Bar laid out in English style—a favourite rendezvous of businessmen in pre-war days.

Seagull Hotel

60 Huangpu Lu; tel. 325-1500; tlx 33603 SISC CN; fax 324-1263

海鸥饭店　黄浦路60号

103 rooms, starting from US$70, suites from US$140. One restaurant serving both Chinese and Western food. Built as an appendage to the International Seamen's Club in 1985, this 14-storey hotel is also open to the general public. Its facilities include rooms for table tennis, chess and *mahjong*. The International Seamen's Club, until recently housed in the former Soviet Consulate, has moved to the Dong Feng Hotel, the Russians having reopened their consulate in their old building.

Seventh Heaven Hotel

627 Nanjing Dong Lu; tel. 322-0777; tlx 33907 BTHQC CN; fax 320-7193

七重天宾馆　南京东路627号

34 rooms, starting from US$50. This small, friendly hotel occupies a fine position on the Nanjing Dong Lu. Situated on the upper floors of the old Wing On Department Store management building, the hotel affords fine views across the city. Owned by the Shanghai TV station.

Sunshine Hotel

2266 Hongqiao Lu; tel. 242-9220; tlx 33451 BTHCQ CN; fax 242-9195

阳光大酒店　虹桥路2266号

131 rooms, starting from US$42, suites from US$70. Four restaurants and a business centre. The five low buildings of the jerry-built hotel, modelled on the traditional south Chinese courtyard house, are showing signs of wear and tear, although fairly recently built.

Yangtze Hotel

740 Hankou Lu; tel. 322-5115; fax 320-6974

扬子饭店　汉口路740号

194 rooms, starting from US$66, suites from US$115. Two Chinese restaurants and business centre. Opened in 1933 and refurbished in 1990, the Yangtze has a good central location, off the Nanjing Xi Lu.

ONE STAR HOTELS
Pujiang Hotel
15 Huangpu Lu; tel. 324-6388; tlx 33921 SMBN CN; fax 306-5147
浦江饭店　黄浦路15号
100 rooms, at US$35 (twin) or around US$5 in dormitory (10 beds per room). One Chinese restaurant. Formerly the elegant Astor House, the building dates from 1911 and overlooks the Huangpu River and Waibaidu Bridge. Partly renovated in 1990, the former ballroom now houses the Shanghai Stock Exchange.

UNCLASSIFIED HOTELS
Cypress Hotel
2419 Hongqiao Lu; tel. 268-8868; tlx 33288 CYH CN; fax 242-3739
龙柏饭店　虹桥路2419号
160 rooms, starting from US$70, suites from US$140. Numerous villas available for long let. Five restaurants, disco, health club. Opened in 1982, the main building, a low-rise block set in a pleasant garden, is showing signs of wear and tear. The Cypress also services the villas built for Shanghai's expatriate community in the grounds behind the hotel. In the grounds can be found Sir Victor Sassoon's old villa, 'Eve's'—a Tudor-style building set on a fine lawn—the scene of some of the wildest parties in the 1930s.

Ruijin Guest House
118 Ruijin Er Lu; tel. 472-5222; tlx 33003 BTHRJ CN; fax 473-2277
瑞金宾馆　瑞金二路118号
47 rooms, prices, from around US$45, on request. The Ruijin is another villa-type guesthouse offering rooms of varying standard in gracious pre-revolution mansions set among well-kept lawns and fountains. There are four villas, the first of which used to house a murky Kuomintang (the Nationalist Party) organization. Long queues are often seen outside the street entrance of the Ruijin's 'French-style' bread shop which is supplied by the guesthouse's own bakery.

Western Suburbs Guesthouse (Xijiao Binguan)
1921 Hongqiao Lu; tel. 219-8800; tlx 33004 BTHHQ CN; fax 433-6641
西郊宾馆　虹桥路1921号
150 rooms, starting from US$120, suites from US$200. Western and Chinese restaurants. Set in beautifully kept grounds, this is a secluded and luxurious guesthouse,

used mainly by official delegations. The complex consists of seven buildings; some were built before 1949 as private houses, other were put up in the 1950s, and the latest addition was completed in 1981. New Building Number Seven contains the presidential suite in which Queen Elizabeth II stayed during her visit to Shanghai in 1986. Under local management.

Xingguo Guest House

72 Xingguo Lu; tel. 433-1220; tlx 33016 BTHXG; fax 251-2145

兴国宾馆　兴国路72号

700 rooms, starting from US$60, suites from US$180. Restaurant, business centre, function room. Another garden-style guesthouse providing accommodation in converted private houses and villas built before the Second World War. The grounds are well looked after, while some of the best rooms offer traditional Chinese furnishings. The complex in its tranquil setting can be found in the southwest of the city.

An array of wines and spirits

Restaurants

Shanghai has over 2000 restaurants and the people of Shanghai delight in eating out. China's economic reform measures have spawned privately-run (*getihu*) businesses at every street corner. Inevitably, some of them are restaurants. They may specialize in one particularly successful line (Cantonese-style roast duck for example), or offer a modest menu (samples are often set out in glasses above the entrance counters, so you can tell at a glance what is available). Look also for westernized names such as Home, Welcome, and others. It would seem that even one's own front room, provided it opens onto the street, can be transformed into a restaurant with the addition of a few 'railway carriage' seats.

Shanghai is amply supplied with freshwater and sea fish and shellfish—eel, carp, shrimps, and most celebrated of all, the *dazha* crabs (better known as Shanghai crabs), in season from October to December. The rich countryside around provides the city with an abundance of fresh vegetables—French beans, peas, Chinese leaves, cabbage, carrots, celery, and a number of delicious greens not encountered in Western cookery. The choice available at any one time, though, depends very much on the season and on the buying habits of the restaurant; many of the vegetables offered in the local markets do not appear on the restaurant table.

As befits a big city with a regionally mixed population, Shanghai's restaurants offer many different types of cuisines, including Sichuan, Canton, Beijing, Moslem and European. Inevitably, the cuisines have been adapted to local taste and ingredients, sometimes to the detriment of their original distinctiveness. This is not the case with the Shanghai breaded pork steak served with a Shanghai sauce (ersatz Lea and Perrin's?), accompanied by potato salad in mayonnaise.

Dishes may be braised, steamed, sautéed, fried in batter or grilled. Ginger, sugar, Shaoxing wine and soy are used extensively in sauces. The Shanghainese are a rice rather than a wheat-eating people, but noodles and steamed dumplings are widely served in addition to rice.

Hardly any tour group will leave China without having sampled a banquet. This can have as many as 15 courses, beginning with a selection of *hors d'oeuvres* of cold vegetables and meats. To order a banquet, one specifies the number of people and chooses from a range of set prices per head. Your hotel can assist you in making reservations.

Fine international cuisine can be experienced at many of the city's top hotels and restaurants—sometimes at prices double those at home. Likewise with beers, wines and spirits at restaurants and bars, especially if they are imported. However local beers are relatively cheap: Tsingtao, China's most famous beer, Steinbrau (brewed in central China) and Reeb (a Swedish assisted project). Local spirits, apart from the increasingly rare Changyu Special Fine Brandy, are not very palatable. The Chinese prefer the schnapps-like *bai jiu*, or 'white spirit', which is a sorghum based clear spirit traditionally used for toasting. *Maotai* is regarded as the finest specimen and commands a high price. The best liqueur cognacs are also very popular with China's new status-seekers.

Visitors should try Shaoxing rice wine, from near Shanghai—rather like *sake* it is usually drunk warm. Traditional Chinese grape wines are rather sweet by Western standards, though the 'China Red' is a palatable Madeira-like concoction. With the assistance of the French and Italians China is now producing some very acceptable Western-style wines, the most popular being Great Wall, Dynasty and Dragon Seal. Try a local Chardonnay if you can. The Shanghai Shenma Vinery Company produces a sound method champenoise called Imperial Brut.

Soft drinks—including Coke, Fanta and Sprite—are readily available, as is a selection of bottled mineral waters including the carbonated Laoshan brand. The tea served in Shanghai, during and after a meal, is usually of the green variety, such as Jasmine (*mouli hua cha*) and Dragon Well (*Longjing*).

(*One word of warning:* If you intend to eat at one of Shanghai's large popular restaurants, such as Sun Ya, ensure you make a booking as flamboyant wedding banquets are a Shanghai obsession.)

CANTONESE CUISINE
Friendship Restaurant (Youyi Jiujia)
Shanghai Exhibition Centre, 1000 Yanan Zhong Lu.
友谊酒家　延安中路1000号上海展览馆
This large restaurant, a joint Shanghai-Hong Kong venture run in the style of Hong Kong restaurants, is a good place for authentic Cantonese foods. *Dim sum*, Cantonese snacks in small baskets or bowls, is wheeled out on trolleys from table to table.

Jade Garden (Cuiyuan) and Ruijin Palace
Windows on the World, 3rd and 27th Floors, Ruijin Building, 205 Maoming Nan Lu.
翠园瑞金宫　茂名南路205号瑞金大厦
Part of a catering group whose establishments include several restaurants in Beijing, the Jade Garden and Ruijin Palace serve what has been bewilderingly dubbed '*nouvelle*' Cantonese cuisine. *Dim sum* is available from 11.30 am–2.30 pm on the 27th-floor Ruijin Palace. These are probably the fanciest restaurants outside of the international hotels in Shanghai.

Hotel Sofitel Hyland Shanghai
505 Nanjing Dong Lu.
海仑宾馆　南京东路505号

The Hai Yue Ting Restaurant on the 5th floor offers authentic Cantonese cuisine prepared by Hong Kong chefs, as well as a large dim sum breakfast buffet at weekends. Open 6 am–9 am; 11.30 am–2.30 pm; 5.30–10.30 pm.

Jinjiang Hotel
59 Maoming Nan Lu.

锦江饭店　茂名南路59号

Both the Butterfly Restaurant, on the first floor, and the Jinyuan (Brocade Garden) Restaurant in the hotel's own 'Food Street' behind the New South Building, specialize in Cantonese cuisine. Cantonese dishes may now also be sampled in the Seafood Restaurant on the ground floor of the New South Building.

Meixin Jiujia
314 Shaanxi Nan Lu.

美心酒家　陕西南路314号

An established and popular Cantonese restaurant which, over time, has adopted something of a Shanghai approach to its cooking of Cantonese food.

Nikko Longbai
2419 Hongqiao Lu.

上海日航龙柏饭店　虹桥路2419号

The Cantonese food in the Tao Li is prepared by chefs from Hong Kong. Opening times are 7 am–9.30 am; 11.30 am–2 pm; 6.30 pm–9.30 pm.

Royal Palace
813 Beijing Dong Lu.

皇府饭店　北京东路813号

The restaurant has a high pedigree, with three chefs previously employed at the Mandarin Hotel in Hong Kong. Reflecting the seasons the menu is changed four times a year. There are a lot of monthly specials such as shark's fin with crab.

Seafood Restaurant (Xijiao Ting)
1330 Nanjing Xi Lu (beside the Shanghai Exhibition Centre).

西角亭　南京西路1330号

This restaurant has a fine reputation among Chinese expatriates in Shanghai. It has become so popular that management can eschew bookings for certain kinds of banquets if they are likely to be too noisy for other diners. Overall high standards are guaranteed by fresh seafood flown in from Canton and a well-trained staff. *Dim sum* is served from 7 am–1.30 pm. Try prawn and beancurd casserole, black bean clam,

Dreaming In The Shanghai Restaurant

I would like to be that elderly Chinese gentleman.
He wears a gold watch with a gold bracelet,
But a shirt without sleeves or tie.
He has good luck moles on his face, but is not disfigured with fortune.
His wife resembles him, but is still a handsome woman,
She has never bound her feet or her belly.
Some of the party are his children, it seems,
And some his grandchildren;
No generation appears to intimidate another.
He is interested in people, without wanting to convert them or pervert
  them.
He eats with gusto, but not with lust;
And he drinks, but is not drunk.
He is content with his age, which has always suited him.
When he discusses a dish with the pretty waitress,
It is the dish he discusses, not the waitress.
The table-cloth is not so clean as to show indifference,
Not so dirty as to signify a lack of manners.
He proposes to pay the bill but knows he will not be allowed to.
He walks to the door like a man who doesn't fret about being respected,
  since he is;
A daughter or granddaughter opens the door for him,
And he thanks her.
It has been a satisfying evening. Tomorrow
Will be a satisfying morning. In between he will sleep satisfactorily.
I guess that for him it is peace in his time.
It would be agreeable to be this Chinese gentleman.

D J Enright

lemon chicken and pan-fried beef. Opening times are 7 am–10.30 am; 11 am–2 pm; 5 pm–8.30 pm; 9 pm–11 pm.

Shanghai Art Salon of Film
127 Maoming Nan Lu.
上海电影文艺沙龙　茂名南路127号
Despite its awkward name this is one of the most popular Hong Kong eateries in the city. As well as an extensive seafood menu (with fresh lobster and crab jetted in from southern China), there is night-club entertainment in the dining room after 9 pm.

Sunya (Xinya)
719 Nanjing Dong Lu.
新雅粤菜馆　南京东路719号
This restaurant on three floors dates from 1928 and has long been a favourite—but it has lost some of its old-world atmosphere as a result of recent renovations.

Xinghualou
343 Fuzhou Lu.
杏花楼　福州路343号
With a history of more than 100 years, this restaurant is well-known for its snake and game banquets. Westerners who baulk at these delicacies will find plenty of other, less exotic Cantonese dishes on the menu.

Beijing And Sichuanese Cuisine
Meilongzheng Jiujia
22, 1081 Lane, Nanjing Xi Lu.
梅龙镇酒家　南京西路1081弄22号
No trip to Shanghai, they say, is complete without a visit to Meilongzheng. Dating from 1938, this is one of the city's most famous restaurants. The rooms are decorated in traditional Chinese style, although renovated in 1988. The restaurant prides itself on its Longyuan beancurd, Imperial Concubine's chicken (*Guifeiji*) and crisp-fried duck (*xiangsu ya*).

Park Hotel
170 Nanjing Xi Lu.
国际饭店　南京西路170号
Like many hotel restaurants in China, the Fengze Lou offers such a comprehensive menu that it appears less a Beijing restaurant than one serving a mixed cuisine. However, the Beijing duck served here cannot be faulted, and the escargots are excellent.

Shanghai Hilton

250 Huashan Lu.

上海静安希尔顿酒店　华山路250号

Sichuan Court (Tianfu Lou) is a plush restaurant, on the 39th floor, ornamented with Chinese paintings, porcelain and reproductions of Ming artifacts. The food here is prepared by a team of chefs from Sichuan and the dishes are 'chilli-rated' as to their hotness. Open from 6 pm–10.30 pm.

Yanyun Lou

755 Nanjing Dong Lu.

燕云楼　南京东路755号

A famous Beijing style restaurant with great Beijing duck and dry fried beef. Opening times are 10.30 am–1.30 pm; 4.30 pm–10.30 pm.

SHANGHAI, YANGZHOU AND NINGBO CUISINES

The cuisines of Shanghai are a variation of the Yangzhou style of cooking, Yangzhou being an old city in Jiangsu, the province immediately to Shanghai's north. Though soya sauce is much used, and also sugar, Yangzhou cooking does not use heavy seasoning. Dishes particularly identified with Shanghai include 'drunken' chicken, 'lion's head' (pork meatballs with cabbage), smoked fish, mock goose, braised eel, and shrimps fried with egg white, but one is now hard put to pinpoint a definitively Shanghainese restaurant in the city. People dining out prefer to sample Sichuan or Cantonese cooking, a bias catered to by the restaurants opened in recent years.

Hotel Sofitel Hyland Shanghai

505 Nanjing Dong Lu.

海仑宾馆　南京东路505号

The Hai Yu Lan Ge Shanghai Restaurant covers the whole range of Shanghai cuisine. Adapted for modern tastes specialities include Crystal Pork Knuckle, eels with garlic and an assortment of hotpot dishes.

The Old Restaurant (Lao Fandian)

242 Fuyou Lu.

老饭店　福佑路242号

As its name suggests, this is a long-established restaurant, specializing in local food. Set in the old Chinese City near the Yu Garden, this rough and ready eating place is on two floors. It is a good place to stop for lunch after a visit to the Yu Garden.

Yangzhou Fandian

308 Nanjing Dong Lu.

扬州饭店　南京东路308号

The Yangzhou seems to live on its reputation, for despite its somewhat disappointing food, the restaurant enjoys good business. Too many choices on the menu undermines any claim that the cooking here is typical of Yangzhou.

Yongjiang Zhuangyuan Lou
162 Xizang Zhong Lu.
勇江状元楼　西藏中路162号
Yongjiang is a river that flows through Ningbo. This restaurant serves the specialities of the area, which are centred on seafood, including the celebrated yellow croaker soup, casserole eel and braised soft-shelled turtle.

MIXED CUISINES
Baigong Restaurant
836 Weihai Lu.
百宫饭店　威海路836号
Of the growing number of privately owned restaurants in Shanghai, the Baigong was one of the earliest to be opened and is included here for its curiosity value as well as for its food. The fare is relatively cheap and good.

Sheraton Hua Ting
1200 Caoxi Bei Lu.
华亭宾馆　漕西北路1200号
Guanyetai, the hotel's roof-top restaurant, offers a wide choice of Cantonese, Sichuan and Shanghai specialities. Service is conscientious.

Jingan Hotel
370 Huashan Lu.
静安宾馆　华山路370号
The Jingan kitchen has a deservedly high reputation, and one can expect to eat well in the eighth-floor dining room of the main block and at the Bright Garden Restaurant of the West Building. But because the latter is so popular, the chefs are often too rushed to perform at their very best, and the waiters get pretty harassed.

Luyangcun
763 Nanjing Dong Lu.
绿杨村　南京东路763号
Luyangcun dates from 1931, and has a menu of Sichuan and Shanghai dishes. One of its specialities are dishes nutritiously enriched with Chinese medicinal herbs, such as its duck and medicinal fungus soup (*dongchong xiacao*). This kind of cooking is not to everyone's taste, and some people have criticized it for being gimmicky.

Peace Hotel

20 Nanjing Dong Lu.

和平饭店　南京东路20号

One eats well in the Dragon-Phoenix Restaurant, where the menus are impressively comprehensive, offering several types of Chinese cuisine. The Peace Hall banquet room is decorated in grand hotel style complete with glittering new chandeliers and a sort of minstrel's gallery. Private banquet rooms are also available.

Shanghai Hilton International

250 Huashan Lu.

上海静安希尔顿酒店　华山路250号

The cuisine of the Shanghai and its surrounding region is combined with Cantonese fare to give a wide range of choice to the diners at the Suiyuan and the Shanghai Express.

WESTERN CUISINE

Champagne Room

Fourth floor, Ruijin Building, 205 Maoming Nan Lu.

世界之窗：香槟厅　茂名南路205号瑞金大厦四楼

This is the European restaurant in the Windows of the World complex. Sunday buffets are available for lunch and dinner.

Garden Hotel Shanghai

58 Maoming Nan Lu.

上海花园酒店　茂名南路58号

The Continental Room is a decadent, classical French restaurant on the 33rd floor of the hotel. Far removed from the tyranny of the city, on offer are business lunches and three course gourmet meals each evening (around 500Rmb). Haute cuisine at its best.

Peace Hotel

20 Nanjing Dong Lu.

和平饭店　南京东路20号

The intimate Peace Grill on the 8th floor is a splendidly restored Art Deco dining room, with Lalique lights and original cutlery. Here you can enjoy caviar from the Ouzoli River, New Zealand sirloin steak and an appetizing selection of salads.

The Red House (Hong Fangzi)

37 Shaanxi Nan Lu.

红房子　陕西南路37号

Dating from 1935, this intriguing anachronism has somehow managed to survive the past 40 years as an entirely European restaurant, offering onion soup, chicken piccata and soufflé Grand Marnier. Renovation in recent years has, alas, robbed it of its earlier atmosphere and the place is no longer evocative of old times, when it was known as Chez Louis.

Shanghai Lan Sheng Hotel

1000 Quyang Lu.
上海兰生大酒店　曲阳路1000号

Under American direction, the Botania restaurant offers a creative menu including pork tenderloin with barley risotto and Chinese dried red plum sauce, and an impressive selection of home-made ice-creams. Open from 5.30 pm–11 pm.

Portman Shangri-La

Second floor, Union Building, 100 Yanan Dong Lu.
香格里拉　延安东路100号联谊大厦二楼

The clientele of this European restaurant is largely drawn from the office block in which it is housed. A joint Shanghai and Singapore concern, the Shangri-La offers a wide-ranging menu from fried rice to fillet steak. The place turns into a disco after 8.30 pm three nights a week.

Sheraton Hua Ting

1200 Caoxi Bei Lu.
华亭喜来登宾馆　漕溪北路1200号

Top-quality restaurants include Anton's, serving French food, and The English Grill Room, specializing in charcoal-grilled steaks and seafood. In addition, there is Luigi's, Shanghai's first Italian restaurant, where pasta and other gastronomic delights are served to the strains of Neapolitan love songs. The menu of the Kafeiting, the coffee shop, also includes a selection of Western dishes.

JAPANESE CUISINE
Nikko Longbai

2451 Hongqiao Lu.
日航龙柏饭店　虹桥路2451号

The hotel's Japanese restaurant, the Benkay, is highly recommended for its impressive array of Japanese specialities. It offers a variety of set meals throughout the day.

Shanghai Hilton International

250 Hua Shan Lu.
上海静安希尔顿酒店　华山路250号

With a spectacular view from the 40th floor, the Miyako Club aims to be Shanghai's premier Japanese restaurant. Most ingredients are flown in from Japan and specialities include beef shabu shabu—a dish made from cattle reared on beer!

Shanghai Centre
1376 Nanjing Xi Lu.
上海中心　南京西路1376号
Located on the 2nd floor of the west tower, the Shiki restaurant offers an Express Japanese set lunch and an extensive evening menu including sushi, sashimi and teriyaki.

You You Restaurant
First floor, Union Building, 100 Yanan Dong Lu.
友友餐厅　延安东路100号联谊大厦一楼
Informal and pleasant venue for Japanese food, as well as cooked fish, spaghetti, hamburger and steak. Less expensive lunch menu.

OTHER TYPES OF RESTAURANTS
Gongdelin Vegetarian Restaurant
43 Huanghe Lu.
功德林素食馆　黄河路43号
A century-old restaurant offering a classic menu in plain front dining rooms or fancier private banquet enclosures complete with heavy mahogany furniture. This is one of the best vegetarian restaurants in the city, and creates mock meat and fish dishes from vegetarian ingredients.

Holiday Inn Crowne Plaza
388 Pan Yu Lu.
上海银星皇冠假日酒店　番禺路388号
The 24 hour Orient Express offers a sumptuous buffet which changes in style each day of the week. Included are dishes from Asia, Germany, Italy and America. A special Sunday Brunch runs from 11.30 am–2.30 pm.

Jinling Curry Chicken Restaurant
370 Jinling Dong Lu.
金陵咖喱鸡饭馆　金陵东路370号
The Jinling opened for business in 1982 and, given the Shanghainese fondness for embracing novelty in any form, the attempt to revive a taste for curries has been

welcomed. Don't go expecting your chicken to be flavoured by a subtle blend of freshly ground spices. You can also have goulash, chops, omelette and macaroni. Besides the dining rooms on two floors, the Jinling also does takeaway lunch boxes. Opening times are 6.30 am–9.30 am; 10 am–4 pm; 5 pm–1 am.

Jinjiang Hotel
59 Maoming Nan Lu.

锦江饭店　茂名南路59号

The Tandoor Restaurant, in the new south building, is Shanghai's first Indian restaurant. The sedate interior of the restaurant is designed on the theme of ancient caravan routes from China through India. Most of the staff are from India and the restaurant specialises in Tandoori dishes from northwest India.

Portman Shangri-La
1376 Nanjing Dong Lu.

波特曼香格里拉酒店　南京东路1376号

The Tea Garden restaurant on the ground floor offers an international buffet for breakfast, lunch and dinner, as well as an extensive menu. A perfect and ever-changing blend of Eastern and Western cuisine is available 24 hours a day.

VIP Satay House (Yuebin Shadie Wu)
849 Huashan Lu.

悦宾沙爹屋　华山路849号

Run by an Indonesian-Chinese manager, this restaurant is popular with tour operators arranging a night out with their groups, so it is essential to book.

SNACKS
There are over 1,800 coffee and pastry shops in Shanghai, selling over 300 kinds of snacks—everything from *youtiao* (deep-fried twisted dough sticks), *dabing* (a large flat bread), to noodles, dumplings and cakes.

For Chinese snacks, you should go to the Old Town, or the **Yu Garden Bazaar**, as it is also called (see page 57). The **Nanxiang Steamed Dumpling Shop** there is certainly worth a visit. The dumplings, stuffed with minced pork, are a speciality of Nanxiang, a small town on the outskirts of Shanghai. Before eating them, dip them in vinegar and shredded ginger. Also worth a visit is the **Lubolang Restaurant** overlooking the pond. There you will find many varieties of pastry, as well as noodles and dumplings, either steamed or deep-fried. Because a visit to the Old Town is a must for Chinese tourists from the provinces, the shops get very crowded and you may have to wait to be served. Another location is Shaanxi Bei Lu. Delicious *shengjian-mantou*, meat-stuffed dumplings which are first steamed and then crisped on a grill can be found at the **Youlian Food Shop** at number 252, a takeaway restaurant boasting a 'Famous and Special Shop' tag awarded by the municipal government.

Over the winter months queues form outside the **Xinchangfa Fruit Shop** at the intersection of Yanan and Chengdu Roads for the best roasted chestnuts in town.

The Shanghainese, who have a very sweet tooth, pride themselves on their Western-style pastries. The ornately decorated cakes in many shades of pastel icing that you can see in the shop windows go down very well as presents. The **bakeries** of the **Jingan** and **Park Hotel** (the latter has a separate entrance at the back of the building) are extremely popular, as is **Laodachang**, a pastry shop plus cafeteria at 877 Huaihai Zhong Lu, which also sells its own brand of ice-cream. Just a few minutes from the Peace Hotel at 145 Nanjing Dong Lu is the **Dong hai** (East Sea) **Café**. Coffee comes with fruit and ice-cream, and from the pastry selection try the bloated lemon meringue pie. Further west at 1001 Nanjing Xi Lu is a branch of **Keisslings**, originally a pre-liberation Austrian enterprise, which carries on the coffee and cake tradition.

For cakes closer to their European models, one must go to the hotel coffee shops and patisseries—the **Kafeiting** and delicatessen at the Sheraton Hua Ting, the **Jinjiang Coffee Shop**, and the **Café de Rêve** in Jinjiang Jie, and the **Hilton** lobby.

Fast food has hit Shanghai. One of the best outlets—for sheer convenience of location, cleanliness, service and choice—is the **Renmin** (open 10.30 am–11 pm) at 226 Nanjing Xi Lu, near the Park Hotel. This is a self-service cafeteria offering meals on a tray, airline-style. A standard meal could be grilled chop, rice and cabbage, plus soup; bacon, eggs and toast are also on offer. Nearly opposite, nearby the entrance to People's Park, is a large **Kentucky Fried Chicken** outlet, with endless queues of locals waiting to be fed. Two minutes walk westwards to the intersection of Huangpi and Nanjing Xi Lu brings one to the **Rong Hua Chicken**, Shanghai's answer to Colonel Sanders. **McDonald's** opened its first 200 seat outlet in Huaihai Zhong Lu in July 1994—of course many more are promised for the future.

Another possibility for fast food is the Sino-Filipino joint venture, the **Yanzhong Hamburger House** at 269-73 Yanan Bei Lu (open 6.30 am–9 am, 10 am–1 pm, 2 pm–6.30 pm). Both lunch boxes and on-the-spot eating are possible. After closing in the evening, the hamburger joint turns into a karaoke bar.

There are countless little markets and stalls around the streets of Shanghai, each offering snacks and specialities. Street food is generally quite good and relatively cheap. Don't be afraid to be adventurous with the new things that you come into contact with.

Useful Addresses

AIRLINES

Air France
Room 32223 International Arrival &
Departure Building, Shanghai
Hongqiao Airport.
Tel. 268-8899 ext. 5325
法国航空公司　上海虹桥机场

All Nippon Airways
Floor 2, Shanghai Centre,
1376 Nanjing Xi Lu.
Tel. 279-7000
全日航空公司　南京西路1376号上海商城

Canadian Airlines International
Floor 6, Jinjiang Tower, 161 Changle Lu.
Tel. 415-3091
加拿大航空公司　长乐路161号新锦江大酒店

China Eastern Airlines
200 Yanan Xi Lu.
Reservations: (International) 247-2255
　　　　　　　　(Domestic) 247-5953
中国东方航空公司　延安西路200号

Dragonair
Room 202, Level 2, West Tower,
Shanghai Centre, 1376 Nanjing Xi Lu.
Tel. 279-8099
港龙航空公司
南京西路1376号上海商城西翼202室

Japan Air Lines
Room 201, Ruijin Building,
205 Maoming Nan Lu.
Tel. 472-3000
Airport Office tel. 268-2084
日本航空公司
茂名南路205号瑞金大厦201室

Korean Air
Room 104–5, Hotel Equatorial,
65 Yanan Xi Lu.
Tel. 248-1555/248-1777
韩国航空公司
延安西路65号贵都酒店104-5室

Lufthansa
Shanghai Hilton International,
250 Huashan Lu.
Tel. 248-1100
德国航空公司
华山路250号上海静安希尔顿酒店

Northwest Airlines Inc
Suite 207, East Podium,
Shanghai Centre,
1376 Nanjing Xi Lu.
Tel. 279-8088
西北航空公司
南京西路1376号上海商城东翼207室

Shanghai Airlines
555 Yanan Zhong Lu.
Tel. 268-0550
上海航空公司　延安中路555号

Singapore Airlines
Room 208, East Wing,
Shanghai Centre,
1376 Nanjing Xi Lu.
Tel. 279-8008
新加坡航空公司
南京西路1376号上海商城东翼208室

United Airlines
Suite 204, West Podium,
Shanghai Centre,
1376 Nanjing Xi Lu.
Tel. 279-8009
美国联合航空公司
南京西路1376号上海商城西翼204室

A Guide To Pronouncing Chinese Names

The official system of Romanization used in China, which the visitor will find on maps, road signs and city shopfronts, is known as *Pinyin*. It is now almost universally adopted by the Western media.

Some visitors may initially encounter some difficulty in pronouncing Romanized Chinese words. In fact many of the sounds correspond to the usual pronunciation of the letters in English. The exceptions are:

Initials

c   is like the *ts* in 'i*ts*'
q   is like the *ch* in '*ch*eese'
x   has no English equivalent, and can best be described as a hissing consonant that lies somewhere between *sh* and *s*. The sound was rendered as *hs* under an earlier transcription system.
z   is like the *ds* in 'fa*ds*'
zh   is unaspirated, and sounds like the *j* in 'jug'.

Finals

a   sounds like '*ah*'
e   is pronounced as in 'h*er*'
i   is pronounced as in 'sk*i*' (written as *yi* when not preceded by an initial consonant). However, in *ci, chi, ri, shi, zi* and *zhi*, the sound represented by the final is quite different and is similar to the *ir* in 's*ir*' but without much stressing of the *r* sound
o   sounds like the *aw* in 'l*aw*'
u   sounds like the *oo* in '*oo*ze'
ü   is pronounced as the German *ü* (written as *yu* when not preceded by an initial consonant). The last two finals are usually written simply as *e* and *u*.

Finals in Combination

When two or more finals are combined, such as in *hao, jiao* and *liu*, each letter retains its sound value as indicated in the list above, but note the following:

ai   is like the *ie* in 'tie'
ei   is like the *ay* in 'bay'
ian   is like the *ien* in 'Vienna'
ie   similar to '*ear*'
ou   is like the *o* in 'code'
uai   sounds like 'why'
uan   is like the *uan* in 'iguana'
      (except when proceeded by *j, q, x* and *y*; in these cases a *u*
      following any of these four consonants is in fact *ü* and *uan* is
      similar to *uen*.)
ue   is like the *ue* in 'duet'
ui   sounds like 'way'

Examples

A few Chinese names are shown below with English phonetic spelling beside them:

Beijing	Bay-jing
Cixi	Tsi-shee
Guilin	Gway-lin
Hangzhou	Hahng-joe
Kangxi	Kahng-shee
Qianlong	Chien-loong
Tiantai	Tien-tie
Xian	Shee-ahn

An apostrophe is used to separate syllables in certain compound-character words to preclude confusion. For example, *Changan* (which can be *chang-an* or *chan-gan*) is sometimes written as *Chang'an*.

Tones

A Chinese syllable consists of not only an initial and a final or finals, but also as tone or pitch of the voice when the words are spoken. In *Pinyin* the four basic tones are marked ¯, ´, ˇ and ˋ. These marks are almost never shown in printed form except in language text.

BANKS

Bank of China (Shanghai branch)
23 Zhongshan Dong Yi Lu.
Tel. 329-1979; fax 323-4872
中国银行（上海分行）　中山东一路23号

ABN AMRO Bank
Peace Hotel, 20 Nanjing Dong Lu.
Tel. 329-9303; fax 329-5199
ABN银行　南京东路20号和平饭店

American Express
Room 206, Retail Plaza, Level 2 West,
Shanghai Centre, 1376 Nanjing Xi Lu.
Tel. 279-8082; fax 279-7183
美国运通国际股份有限公司
南京西路1376号上海商城西翼206室

Australia & New Zealand Banking Group Ltd
201 A West Wing Office Complex,
Hotel Equatorial, 65 Yanan Xi Lu.
Tel. 248-8877; fax 248-0080
澳新银行上海分行　延安西路65号贵都大饭店综合办公楼西翼201A室

Bank of America
Room 104–107A Union Building, 100 Yanan Dong Lu.
Tel. 329-2828; fax 320-1297
美国美洲银行
延安东路100号联谊大厦104-107A室

Bank of Tokyo
Room 1207 Ruijin Building,
205 Maoming Nan Lu.
Tel. 433-4036; fax 433-4175/7871
东京银行　茂名南路205号瑞金大厦1207室

Banque Indosuez
Rm 502–5, Union Building,
100 Yanan Dong Lu.

Tel. 329-2228; fax 329-2911
法国东方汇理苏伊士银行
延安东路100号联谊大厦502-5室

Barclays Bank
Suite 530 West Podium,
Shanghai Centre, 1376 Nanjing Xi Lu.
Tel. 279-8279; fax 279-8239
栢克莱银行
南京西路1376号上海商城西翼530室

Chase Manhattan Bank
203A Shanghai Centre.
1376 Nanjing Xi Lu.
Tel./fax 279-7023
美国大通银行
南京西路1376号上海商城203A室

Citibank
Floor 5, Union Building,
100 Yanan Dong Lu.
Tel. 329-1335
美国花旗银行
延安东路100号联谊大厦5楼

Credit Lyonnais
Suite 715, West Podium, Shanghai Centre, 1376 Nanjing Xi Lu.
Tel. 279-8661; fax 279-8662
法国里昂信贷银行上海分行
南京西路1376号上海商城西翼715室

Fuji Bank
Rm 1101 Ruijin Building,
205 Maoming Nan Lu.
Tel. 433-0317
富士银行　茂名南路205号瑞金大厦1101室

Hang Seng Bank
Room 1301 Ruijin Building,
205 Maoming Nan Lu.

Tel. 472-8781; fax 472-8776
恒生银行　茂名南路205号瑞金大厦1301室

The Hongkong and Shanghai Banking Corporation
185 Yuanmingyuan Lu.
Tel. 321-0811/329-1775; fax 329-1659
香港上海汇丰银行　圆明园路185号

Mitsubishi Bank
Rm 2404 Ruijin Building,
205 Maoming Nan Lu.
Tel. 472-0882
三菱银行　茂名南路205号瑞金大厦2404室

Standard Chartered Bank
Level 7, Shanghai Centre,
1376 Nanjing Xi Lu.
Tel. 279-8823; fax 279-8813
标准渣打（麦加利）银行
南京西路1376号上海商城7座

CONSULATES
Australia
17 Fuxing Xi Lu.
Tel. 433-4604; fax 433-1732
澳大利亚领事馆　复兴西路17号

Belgium
1375 Huaihai Zhong Lu,
Tel. 433-4466
比利时领事馆　淮海中路1375号

Canada
Suite 604, West Tower,
Shanghai Centre,
1376 Nanjing Xi Lu.
Tel. 279-8400; fax 279-8401
加拿大领事馆
南京西路1376号上海商城西翼604室

CIS
20 Huangpu Lu.
Tel. 324-2682/324-8383
俄罗斯独联体领事馆　黄埔路20号

Cuba
55 Loushanguan Lu.
Tel. 275-3078
古巴领事馆　娄山关路55号

France
1375 Huaihai Zhong Lu.
Tel. 437-7414; fax 433-9437
法国领事馆　淮海中路1375号

Germany
151 Yongfu Lu.
Tel. 433-6951; fax 471-4448
德国领事馆　永福路151号

Great Britain
244 Yongfu Lu.
Tel. 433-0508; fax 433-3115
英国领事馆　永福路224号

India
Shanghai International Trade Centre,
2200 Yanan Xi Lu.
Tel. 275-8886
印度领事馆　延安西路2200号上海国贸中心

Iran
Room 2307, Ruijin Building,
205 Maoming Nan Lu.
Tel. 472-1389
依朗领事馆　茂名南路205号瑞金大厦2307室

Italy
127 Wuyi Lu.
Tel. 252-4373
意大利领事馆　武夷路127号

Japan
1517 Huaihai Zhong Lu.
Tel. 433-6639; fax 433-1008
日本领事馆　淮海中路1517号

New Zealand
1375 Huaihai Zhong Lu.
Tel. 433-2230
新西兰领事馆　淮海中路1375号

Poland
618 Jianguo Xi Lu.
Tel. 433-9376/433-9288
波兰领事馆　建国西路618号

Republic of Korea
Shanghai International Trade Centre,
2200 Yanan Xi Lu.
Tel. 219-6417
韩国共和国领事馆　延安西路2200号上海
国贸中心

Singapore
400 Wulumuqi Zhong Lu.
Tel. 433-1362; fax 433-4150
新加坡领事馆　乌鲁木齐中路400号

USA
1469 Huaihai Zhong Lu,
Tel. 433-6880; fax 433-4122
美国领事馆　淮海中路1469号

MUSEUMS
Shanghai Art Museum
456 Nanjing Xi Lu.
上海美术博物馆　南京西路456号

Shanghai History Museum
1286 Hongqiao Lu.
上海历史博物馆　虹桥路1286号

Shanghai Museum (open late 1995)
Renmin Square
上海博物馆　人民广场

Shanghai Natural History Museum
260 Yanan Dong Lu.
上海自然博物馆　延安东路260号

CONVENTION AND EXHIBITION VENUES

The following hotels have facilities of
international standard for hosting
conferences, meetings and exhibitions:
**Garden, Hilton, Jinjiang Tower,
Portman Shangri-La, Sheraton Hua
Ting, Westin, Yangtze New World,
Lan Sheng, J C Mandarin, Nikko
Longbai.**

Shanghai Exhibition Centre
1000 Yanan Zhong Lu.
Tel. 279-0279; fax 247-4246
上海展览馆　延安中路1000号

**INTEX (International Exhibition)
Shanghai**
88 Loushanguan Lu.
Tel. 275-8000; fax 275-7210
上海国际展览馆　娄山关路88号

PARKS
Fuxing Park
105 Yandang Lu.
复兴公园　雁荡路105号

Guilin Park
1 Guilin Lu.
桂林公园　桂林路1号

Hongkou Park
146 Dongjiangwang Lu.
虹口公园　东江湾路146号

Huangpu Park
18 Zhongshan Dong Yi Lu.
黄埔公园　中山东一路18号

Renmin Park
Nanjing Xi Lu and Xizang Zhong Lu.
人民公园　南京西路西藏中路

Zhongshan Park
Changning Lu.
中山公园　长宁路

POST AND TELECOMMUNICATIONS
Shanghai Central Post Office
359 Tiantong Lu.
上海市邮政局　天潼路359路

**Shanghai Telecommunications
Building** (Service Office)
1122 Yanan Dong Lu.
上海电信大楼营业处　延安东路1122号

Shanghai Telegraph Office (Main
branch)
30 Nanjing Dong Lu.
上海市电报局（总局）南京东路30号

SHOPS
ANTIQUES, ARTS AND CRAFTS
**Chong Shin (Chuangxin) Old Arts
and Crafts Store**
1297 Huaihai Lu.
创新古玩店　准海路1297号

Friendship Store
40 Beijing Dong Lu.
友谊商店　北京东路40号

Hualian Commercial Building
634 Nanjing Dong Lu.
华联商厦　南京东路634号

Guohua Porcelain Store
550 Nanjing Dong Lu.
国华瓷器商店　南京东路550号

Old Town Embroidery Shop
21 Yuyuan Xin Lu.
南市刺绣商店　豫园新路21号

Old Town Handicraft Store
21 Yicheng Lu.
南市工艺品商店　邑城路21号

Shaanxi Old Ware Store
557 Yanan Zhong Lu.
陕西旧货店　延安中路557号

Shanghai Antiques and Curios Store
218–226 Guangdong Lu.
上海文物商店　广东路218-226号

**Shanghai Jingdezhen Porcelain
Store**
1175 Nanjing Xi Lu.
上海景德镇艺术瓷器服务部　南京西路
1175号

Yuhua Arts and Crafts Store
929–935 Huaihai Zhong Lu.
玉华工艺商店　准海中路929-935号

SPECIALITY SHOPS
**Guan Long Photographic Supplies
Store**
190 Nanjing Dong Lu.
冠龙照相材料商店　南京东路190号

Shanghai Arts and Crafts Jewellery and Jade Ware Store
438 Nanjing Dong Lu.
上海市珠宝玉器商店　南京东路438号

Shanghai Stamps Company
244 Nanjing Dong Lu.
上海邮票公司　南京东路244号

Tiehuaxuan Pottery Shop
Yu Garden Bazaar
铁画轩紫砂陶瓷店　豫园商场

Wang Sin Kee (Wang Xingji) Fan Shop
782 Nanjing Dong Lu.
王星记扇庄　南京东路782号

Wanli Walking Stick Shop
Yu Garden Bazaar.
万里手杖店　豫园商场

Zhang Xiaoquan Scissors Shop
490 Nanjing Dong Lu.
张小泉剪刀店　南京东路490号

BOOKS AND MAGAZINES
China Classic Bookstore
424 Fuzhou Lu.
古籍书店　福州路424号

Foreign Languages Bookstore
380 & 390 Fuzhou Lu.
外文书店　福州路380与390号

Foreign Languages Bookstore
Jinjiang Hotel Branch,
59 Maoming Nan Lu.
外文书店　锦江饭店分店茂名南路59号

Foreign Languages Bookstore (Old books section)
201 Shandong Zhong Lu.
外文书日店旧书门市部　山东中路201号

Shanghai Bookstore
401–411 Fuzhou Lu.
上海书店　福州路401-411号

Shanghai Classics Bookstore
438 Fuzhou Lu.
上海古籍书店　福州路438号

Xinhua Bookstore
345 Nanjing Dong Lu.
新华书店　南京东路345号

CHINESE MEDICINES
Cai Tongde
320 Nanjing Dong Lu.
蔡同德堂药号　南京东路320号

Lei Yun Shang
719 Nanjing Xi Lu.
雷允上药店　南京西路719号

DEPARTMENT STORES
Friendship Store
40 Beijing Dong Lu.
友谊商店　北京东路40号

Hualian Department Store
635 Nanjing Dong Lu.
华联商厦　南京东路635号

Isetan
527 Huaihai Zhong Lu.
伊势丹　淮海中路527号

Jinjiang Dickson Center
400 Changle Lu.
锦光迪生中心　长乐路400号

Maison Mode
1312 Huaihai Zhong Lu.
美美百货商店　淮海中路1312号

Manhattan Plaza
463–477 Nanjing Dong Lu.
曼克顿广场　南京东路463-477号

Oriental Shopping Centre
8 Caoxi Bei Lu,
Xujiahui Commercial Plaza.
东方商店中心　漕溪北路8号

Shanghai No. 1 Department Store
830 Nanjing Dong Lu.
上海第一百货商店　南京东路830号

Shui Hing
152 Huaihai Zhong Lu.
瑞兴公司　淮海中路152号

Sincere Department Store
463–477 Nanjing Dong Lu.
先施百货公司　南京东路463-477号

Tai Ping Yang Department Store
932 Hengshan Lu,
Xujiahui Commercial Plaza.
太平洋百货公司　恒山路932号

Wings Department Store
869 Nanjing Xi Lu.
永安百货公司　南京西路869号

PAINTING AND CALLIGRAPHY

Wenfang Sibao
Jinjiang Hotel,
59 Maoming Nan Lu.
文房四室　茂名南路59号锦江饭店

SUPERMARKETS
Jessica
Jinjiang Hotel,
59 Maoming Nan Lu.
吉佳超级市场　茂名南路59号锦江饭店

Wellcome
Shanghai Centre, 1376 Nanjing Xi Lu.
惠康超级市场　南京西路1376号上海商城

TRAVEL AND TRANSPORT
China International Travel Service (CITS)
21/22F, Guangming Building,
2 Jinling Xi Lu.
Tel. 321-7200; fax 329-1788
中国国际旅行社　金陵西路2号

CITS Multi-Service Departments (ticketing/tours)
3/F Guangming Building,
2 Jinling Xi Lu.
Tel. 321-7200/323-8750
中旅社票务部　金陵西路2号
and at the following hotels:
Jinjiang: Tel. 256-2857/215-4440
Sheraton Hua Ting: Tel. 481-1116
Peace (North Wing): Tel. 323-4067
Shanghai Centre: Tel. 279-8061
Rainbow: Tel. 275-3756

China Travel Service (CTS)
881 Yanan Zhong Lu.
Tel. 247-8888; fax 247-5521
中国旅行社　延安中路881号

China Youth Travel Service (CYTS)

2 Hengshan Lu.
Tel. 433-1826; fax 433-0507
中国青年旅行社　衡山路2号

Friendship Taxi Company

849 Yanan Zhong Lu. Tel. 258-4584
友谊汽车服务公司　延安中路849号

Jinjiang Tours

Room 1001, 27/F Union Building,
100 Yanan Dong Lu.
Tel. 326-5050/326-5095
上海市锦江旅游有限公司
延安东路100号联谊大厦27楼1001室

Long-distance Bus Station

Junction of Qiujiang and Gongxing Lu.
长途汽车站　虬江路公兴路口

Northern Bus Station

Junction of Gonghexin
and Zhongshan Bei Lu.
北区汽车站　共和新路中山北路口

Shanghai Harbour Passenger Transport Terminal

1 Jinling Dong Lu.
Tel. 326-0050
上海港客运总站　金陵东路1号

Shanghai (Hongqiao) International Airport

Tel. (flight enquiries) 253-6530
上海虹桥国际飞机场

Shanghai Municipal Tourism Administration

Hua Ting Guest House,
2525 Zhongshan Xi Lu.
Tel. 439-1869/1818 ext. 2407;
fax 439-1519
上海市旅游行政局
中山西路2525号华亭宾馆

Shanghai Port Passengers General Terminal, International passengers

1 Taiping Street, Dongdaming Lu.
Tel. 541-9529
上海港客运总站国际客运站
东大名路太平街1号

Shanghai Railway Station

Hengfeng Bei Lu, Tianmu Xi Lu.
Tel. 325-3030/317-9234
上海火车站　天目西路恒丰北路

Shanghai Taxi Corporation

920 Nanjing Xi Lu.
Tel. 258-0000
上海出租汽车　南京西路920号

Western Bus Station

240 Caoxi Bei Lu.
西区汽车站　漕溪北路240号

China Travel Service (HK)

Head Office. 78 Connaught Road
Central, Hong Kong.
Tel. 2853-3533
香港中国旅行社　香港中环干诺道中78号

MISCELLANEOUS

China Council for the Promotion of International Trade, Shanghai Sub-Council

33 Zhongshan Dong Yi Lu, Tel. 323-2348
中国国际贸易促进委员会上海市分会
中山东一路33号

DHL Parcel Delivery

603 Zhongshan Nan Lu.
Tel. 376-2454/0020; tlx 337106 DHLSH;
fax 376-0115
敦豪国际航空快件有限公司
中山南路630号

Fudan University
220 Handan Lu.
Tel. 549-1128; fax 326-9848
复旦大学 邯郸路220号

Jiaotong University
1954 Huashan Lu.
Tel. 431-0310; fax 433-0892
交通大学 华山路1954号

Public Security Bureau
Foreigners Section (open 9 am–11 am;
2 pm–5.30 pm)
210 Hankou Lu.
Tel. 321-5380
公安局外事科 汉口路210号

Shanghai Conservatory of Music
20 Fenyang Lu.
Tel. 437-0137 or 433-0536
上海音乐学院 分阳路20号

Shanghai Foreign Economic Relations and Trade Commission (SMERT)
New Town Mansion,
55 Loushanguan Lu. Tel. 275-1589
上海市对外经济贸易委员会
娄山关路55号新虹桥大厦

Shanghai Foreign Investment Commission
New Town Mansion,
55 Loushanguan Lu. Tel. 275-5192
上海市对外投资委员会
娄山关路55号新虹桥大厦

Shanghai Pudong New Area Administration
141 Pudong Jie. Tel. 878-8388
上海市浦东新区管理委员会 浦东大道141号

UPS Parcels
304A, Hotel Equatorial, 65 Yanan Xi Lu.
Tel. 248-6060/8621
延安西路65号贵都大饭店304A室

ESSENTIAL TELEPHONE NUMBERS

Ambulance	120
Police	321-3030
Fire	119
Flight Information:	
International	247-2255
Domestic	247-5953
Train Information	317-9234
Ferry Information	326-1261
Tourist Information	439-1818
Directory Assistance	114
International	
Directory Enquiries	116
Telephone Fault	112
Time	117
Weather	121

Practical information, such as telephone numbers, opening hours, hotel and restaurant prices *etc.*, is inevitably subject to being quickly outdated by changes or inflation, especially in somewhere like Shanghai. Therefore we always welcome updates, suggestions, corrections and guidebook users' comments. Please write to:

The Guidebook Company Ltd,
G/F, 15 Lower Kai Yuen Lane,
North Point,
Hong Kong.

An Actress Invited To The Party

The Film Studio was a palace of displayed slogans. It was surrounded by dark-red maple trees. The leaves were like joined hands. They blocked my view. The studio walls were painted white with red slogans written on them. 'Long live Chairman Mao's revolutionary arts' policy!' 'Salute to our greatest standard-bearer, Comrade Jiang Ching!'

I presented a sealed official letter to the studio security guard. He told me to wait as he went inside. A few minutes later a man and a woman appeared in a hallway. They threw themselves at me enthusiastically. The man introduced himself as Sound of Rain, the head of the studio acting department, the woman as Soviet Wong, his assistant. They picked up my luggage and asked me to follow them into the studio.

We passed through a series of gates. The sun was shining through the maple leaves. The leaves were spreading their pinkish rays on to the dustless pavement. The workers walking underneath the maple trees were covered in reddish light. They greeted us with flattery.

Sound of Rain had a pumpkin head with fat cheeks sagging on the sides. Soviet Wong had a face of an ancient beauty. She had slanting eyes, a long nose, a cherry-shaped mouth and extremely fine skin. She was about forty. It was the way she moved, her elegance drew me in. She spoke perfect Mandarin. She had a silky voice. Sound of Rain spoke of Soviet Wong. He said that she was a graduate from the Shanghai Film Acting School in the fifties and was an extremely talented actress. Sound of Rain said that I should be proud that I would have more than one instructor. Sound of Rain said it was Madam Mao Comrade Jiang Ching's order. Soviet Wong said that she was very happy to receive the assignment of being in charge of teaching me. I asked what I would be learning. She said I would be taking intensive classes in politics and acting. I asked if she would do any acting with us. She went silent. Her lips tightened and her head lowered. A lump of hair fell on her face. Her steps slowed down. The Revolution's needs are my needs, she said stiffly. Her resentment spat out between her teeth. She looked clearly unhappy. Flinging back her hair, she quickly sped up to catch Sound of Rain. Her graceful back bent slightly to the right side. She pretended to be very happy. She must be as durable as bamboo—capable of bending in all directions in the wind. I walked carefully, watching my own steps.

Soviet Wong walked half a step behind Sound of Rain, never overtaking him or lagging behind him one step. They both wore blue Mao jackets with collars buttoned tightly to the neck. They nodded, Sound of Rain first, then Soviet Wong, at the workers who passed by. They paid the workers full-scale smiles. The smile made me nervous although it was the most admired smile in the country. It was the smile that Mao had been promoting with the slogan, 'One must treat one's comrades with the warmth of spring.' Lu at Red Fire Farm was an expert at that type of smile.

Finally, we arrived at an abandoned studio set. It was the size of a stadium engulfed by foot-high weeds. As we made a sharp turn, a single little blue house appeared in front of me. It was an old house with a cement sink on the ground. Wild plants climbed around the sink. This is where you girls stay, said Soviet Wong. This used to be an old film set, Sound of Rain explained. There are more living quarters behind the house. It was built as a horse shed for films. We had it converted into a living space for the boys chosen. Twenty-five of you are assigned to live and work in this area. You will be guarded. No visits to or from families except the second Sunday morning of the month. Anyone who breaks the rules will be eliminated. We want no outside influence. Absolutely none, Soviet Wong echoed. My thoughts turned to Yan.

What about letters? I asked. What's so urgent about writing letters? Soviet Wong suddenly turned to me, suspicion rising in her voice. Her long thin eyebrows twisted into a knot in the middle. I reacted quickly to this sign of danger. I said, Oh, nothing, I was just asking.

She did not believe me. I could tell that she went on with her own thinking. You have dark circles under your eyes, which shows that you don't sleep well. What's your problem? We hope your promise to the party was not a fake one. She turned to Sound of Rain and said, We must take preventative measures against possible calamities.

I was offended but I knew not to show my feelings. The engine of my brain sped up to its limit. Nothing is more urgent than the assignment I have been given, I said, trying to sound sincere. It might be my late Mao study habit that causes the dark circles around my eyes. She asked, Why don't you tell us the name of the person you would like to write to so we can check to make sure that it is good for you to keep the correspondence?

Anchee Min, *Red Azalea*

Through The Eyes Of Poets

Seen from the river, towering above their couchant guardian warships, the semi-skyscrapers of the Bund present, impressively, the façade of a great city. But it is only a façade; behind them is a sordid and shabby mob of smaller buildings. Nowhere a fine avenue, a spacious park, an imposing central square. Nowhere anything civil at all. Nevertheless the tired or lustful business man will find here everything to gratify his desires. You can buy an electric razor, or a French dinner, or a well-cut suit. You can attend race-meetings, baseball games, football matches. You can see the latest American films. If you want girls, or boys, you can have them, at all prices, in the bath-houses and the brothels. If you want opium you can smoke it in the best company, served on a tray, like afternoon tea. Good wine is difficult to obtain in the climate, but there is enough whisky and gin to float a fleet of battleships. The jeweller and the antique-dealer await your orders, and their charges will make you imagine yourself back on Fifth Avenue or in Bond Street. Finally, if you ever repent, there are churches and chapels of all denominations.

W H Auden and Christopher Isherwood, *Journey to a War*

Money Changers

Already estimates put the number of Chinese Kuanye (cash god) million-aires at 4 to 5 million. And then there were all the geti hu (private entrepreneurs) whose capitalist-style businesses formed the backbone of the burgeoning new middle class; the dakuan (big bucks) high rollers; the dahu (big players) from the stock market; and the huanqiande (money changers) in the streets. Each of Nanjing East Road's many money changers had a doorway or arcade entrance from which they worked their 'territory.' As soon as a foreigner appeared on their stretch of the street, they darted out from their hiding places like trout streaking out from under rocks to strike at floating insects. 'Yoooo lika sharnsha manee? OK!' one man dressed in a white, Tom Wolfe-like suit hissed at me as I crossed the Henan Road. Then doing an adept little two-step beside me as I edged back up onto the sidewalk, he repeated his proposition over and over again, sotto voce, like a mantra. Only seconds after Tom Wolfe broke off contact, another money changer— this one sporting a studied coiffure, a silk windbreaker, and a Marlboro clamped between his nicotine-stained teeth—materialized beside me. Like a pimp, he shadowed me the rest of the way down the block, making his whispered entreaties in the same fractured English. No sooner had he vanished than a third struck. All of these hustlers were part of a Mafia-like syndicate that was doing tens of millions of dollars in black-market currency exchanges. All that I could think was that if any of them dared to ply their trade in Shanghai's streets in 1975, they would have ended up in prison. But in the midst of this neon energy, prisons, especially the idea of political prisoners, seemed utterly remote.

Orville Schell, *Mandate of Heaven*

Index Of Places

NOTES